PAY TO THE ORDER OF
CITYWIDE BANK OF APPLEWOOD
WHEAT RIDGE, COLO. 80033
⑆107002231⑆
FOR DEPOSIT ONLY
ELEGANT GLASS ANTIQUES
046017 30

Ruby Glass
of the
20th Century

D0580471

by Naomi L. Over

A. 8¼" Rose Wreath oil lamp. Made by Pittsburgh Lamp, Brass and Glass Company; converted to electric.

B. Footed tumbler made by Anchor Hocking in 1938, Line 888.

C. #888 Plume 3 piece epergne. Made by Paden City in the 1930's.

D. #121 Swirl 14" cornucopia vase. This was made in three shapes, numbered 1, 2, 3, differing in the position into which the tail was tooled. All three varieties were available in 1943. In 1951 only the #2 shape in clear was being made by the United States Glass Company about 1957, as #121-117.

Copyright 1990
by Antique Publications

Hardbound I.S.B.N. #0-915410-67-2
Softbound I.S.B.N. #0-915410-68-0

Additional copies may be ordered from:

ANTIQUE PUBLICATIONS
P.O. Box 553
Marietta, Ohio 45750

This book is dedicated to my beloved husband John, for without him I would never have spent so many beautiful hours enjoying Ruby glass.

I hope by sharing these stories and information, my hobby will be as enjoyable for all of you as my collection of Ruby glass is to me.

Naomi L. Over was born and reared in Colorado. She has three daughters and eight grandchildren. She taught in the public schools for 30 years in adult education and high school. She has collected Ruby glass for over 25 years.

Here is how this book got started:

My Aunt ran a grocery store in Denver, and the first pieces I received were 8 glasses that you will see a sample of one on the cover. They were given as premiums with groceries.

I married John Over 25 years ago, and he discovered the glasses on a shelf wrapped in a 1932 newpaper. He fell in love with the beautiful Ruby color, and that started my collection. I now have over 5000 pieces ... and I'm still looking!

I would like to thank my family for all the beautiful pieces of Ruby glass they have bought for me. To my daughter Marlena, who spent thousands of hours helping me put this book together--I would not have made it without you. I thank Zeta and Charlie Todd for their expertise and knowledge of Ruby glass. And thanks, also, to Dave Richardson for the beautiful pictures you are about to see.

Table of Contents

RUBY AND GOLD: FACT OR FICTION?

One of the most interesting and pervasive folktales in American glassmaking is the story of the glassmaker who threw (or accidentally dropped) gold coins into a batch of crystal glass. As if by magic, the glass turned into a beautiful ruby color, and the glassmaker later lined his pockets with gold as the public clamored for more and more of the secretive ruby glass! A variation of this story, repeated in Lura Woodside Watkins' Cambridge Glass (1930), finds a glassmaker's gold ring fueling the miracle.

In an article for the Journal of Glass Studies (1970) entitled "Metallic Gold and Ruby Glass," R. G. Newton set out to prove or disprove these seemingly fanciful accounts of ruby glass making. He was well aware of glassworkers who insisted that they had seen, with their own eyes, the tossing of gold coins into the molten glass batches which produced ruby ware.

After an exhaustive survey of glassmakers' batch books and many queries to glass technologists, Newton concluded that gold was indeed present in ruby glass batches, but that the gold must be dissolved in a mixture of two powerful acids called aqua regia. This mixture is hazardous to handle, and it holds the gold in what is called a colloidal suspension. One batch book quoted by Newton called it "fulminating gold."

Frank M. Fenton recalls many conversations about the use of gold in making ruby glass, and he notes that ruby glasses in the nineteenth and first quarter of the twentieth century were invariably produced by blowing operations. Ruby glass is said to "strike," or acquire its desired color, upon careful reheating at a glory hole. Much of the time, ruby glass was covered or "cased" with clear glass. Those glassworkers who gathered the first, small amount of ruby batch were called core gatherers.

In the 1890s, the American Flint Glass Workers Union had special provisions which applied to all workers involved in producing ruby glassware: they were required to produce 10% fewer pieces than shops working crystal or other colors, simply because of the time needed to reheat articles at the glory hole to strike the desired ruby color. The famous glassmaker Harry Northwood was particularly fond of ruby glassware, and many articles produced at his factories in Martins Ferry, OH, and Ellwood City and Indiana, PA, are called "cranberry" today. They were made from ruby batches containing gold dissolved in aqua regia.

Even contemporary glassmakers have had their problems with ruby glass. In working with Frank M. Fenton on the book Fenton Glass: The Third Twenty-Five Years, I puzzled over pieces that seemed more orange than ruby or vice versa. Mr. Fenton explained that ruby is a heat-sensitive glass, and that the line between ruby and orange is a thins one, indeed.

Most recently, glass plants have developed ruby glass batches which depend upon the chemical element Selenium for their color properties. These batches can be pressed successfully, and many of the pressed ware articles shown in this book were surely made from Selenium-based rather than from gold-based ruby.

Nonetheless, hope dies hard, and some will, no doubt, remain beguiled by the romantic story of the gold coins and the miracle of ruby glass. Newton also mentions that the addition of small amounts of gold coin would do no harm to a well-prepared batch using gold in aqua regia, and he suggests that the addition of a coin or two may have been for purposes of superstition.

Finally, Newton and his colleagues actually prepared several batches of molten glass, adding gold to the mixtures. The result: a small deposit or residue of gold at the bottom of the pot, but no ruby glass!

James Measell, Director
Glass History Research
Antique Publications

DESCRIPTION OF COLOR PAGES

Figures 1-12: **Blenko Glass Company,** Milton, West Virginia

In 1930, when this factory began making hand-blown tableware, red glass was in production. It had been prominent for several years in the glass which the Blenkos, under the name of Eureka Art Glass Company, had been making for stained glass windows. Deep red, called ruby by the company, has been in Blenko's line apparently much of the time since, and, as recently as 1984, though it did not appear in the 1970 catalogue. Tangarine, a red with yellow shading (sometimes an orange color throughout), may have been made as early as the 1950s; it was definitely in the Blenko catalogue by 1970, and last appeared there in 1984.

All of the shapes pictured here appeared in Blenko's 1981 catalogue.

1. Ruby #404M vase, 11" by 8¼". The letters S, M, and L following Blenko shape numbers indicate size, and apparently stand for small, medium, and large. This #404 shape had been made much earlier than 1981, possibly as early as 1940.

2. Ruby #939P pitcher, 14" tall, a shape reportedly being made by about 1952.

3. Ruby decanter, 13" tall.

4. Tangerine #37 decanter, 13¼" tall, a shape reportedly introduced in 1937, still shown in the 1970 catalogue.

5. Ruby bowl, shape #3744 (possibly #3744X), height 3¼". This shape also appeared in the 1970 catalogue.

6. Basket, yellow (possibly Wheat) handle on 4½" high ruby body.

7. #7634 candlestick, height 3", ruby with yellow, (possibly Wheat) handle. This shape appeared in the Blenko catalogues by 1980 and as recently as 1985.

8. Ruby pitcher, height 6¾".

9. Ruby #39, (possibly #39L) vase, height 5½". This shape has been made in several sizes.

10. Ruby #3750 pitcher. This shape has been made in at least three sizes, offered by Blenko as 40, 16, and 8 ounce (L, M, and S respectively).

11. Ruby #51 bubble, 5". This shape, made in at least three sizes, was made apparently as early as the mid-1930s.

12. #76A or #711A snowman paperweight, height 5½". Made in 1979 and at least as late as 1983; crystal with red (Blenko's color description) hat, nose, and buttons.

13, 14. Newport plates, 8½" and 14". Maker unknown. See also Figure 407. This pattern was advertised as Newport by Pitman-Dreitzer and Company, a New York distributor. A 1935 advertisement illustrating these and other table items offered the pattern in "Crystal, Ruby, Blue, Amethyst, Amber, Evergreen, Rose." This should not be confused with the Newport patterns of the Hazel-Atlas Glass Company and the United States Glass Company; they do not resemble this one, and neither is known in red.

Figures 15, 18, 20-22, 25-43, 45-53: **Cambridge Glass Company,** Cambridge, Ohio.

Cambridge, as one of the country's largest producers of handmade glass, first placed its red glass, called Carmen, on the market in 1931. It was advertised through the 1930s, and was still in production in 1942. It was again offered in the 1950s, apparently having been dropped for a period and reintroduced in 1949 or 1950.

For additional Cambridge items, see Figures 138, 291, 394 and 490.

15. #3400/4 12" four-toed bowl, an item made from 1930 to at least 1950. The 3400 line of dinnerware was a large and popular one, more of ten found in colors other than red. See also Figures 22, 25, 28-32.

16. Maker unknown. Decanter, dumbell-shaped with metal cap, 13" long, possibly 1935-1940.

17. Viking Glass Company's #1007 one-light "Flowerlite," 5", consisting of a three-toed cupped bowl and a clear flower block with a candle well in its center. This shape was evidently being made in 1952 or later, as it shared a catalogue page with a piece of Viking's #5200 Princess pattern, reportedly introduced in 1952.

18. "Game Set" of four tumblers (10-ounce, per catalogue), clear with colored feet: Ebony spade and club, Carmen diamond and heart. This set was introduced in 1949 or 1950.

19. Summit Art Glass Company's 13" Swan, made in 1986 from the mold formerly used by Cambridge Glass Company for its #1045 13" Swan. This style, with smooth feathers, was made by Cambridge around 1940; the earliest Cambridge examples, as made from 1928 to at least 1930, have much detail in the feathers. In 1930, this size was offered as a "Table Decoration" in which a flower block could be used. The red color in this Summit piece is poorly developed. It must be remembered, however, that amber shading can be found in Cambridge Carmen pieces, including Swans. This example was purchased at the Summit factory.

20. #1043 Swan, 8½". This size also had finely detailed feathers originally, from 1928 to at least 1933, but by 1949 had been changed to the smooth-feathered type shown here, which evidently was made at least as late as 1956. It is known to have been offered in Carmen in 1950. In 1930, Cambridge suggested this size of Swan for use as a celery holder, for bon bons, or as a centerpiece with a flower block.

21. #1040 Swan, 3", in the last of three successively less detailed versions in which Cambridge made it, beginning in 1928. This variety, made 1950-1956, was offered in Carmen in 1950. Cambridge called the earliest version an "Individual Nut or Mint" in 1930; later ones were sometimes called ash trays. The type shown here has been reproduced since 1973 or earlier; Mosser Glass, of Cambridge, Ohio, has made it as #118

Swan salt dip, in various colors. Some Mosser examples are marked with an M.

22. #3400/71 3" individual nut, 1931-1950. The mold for this was used about 1966 by Imperial Glass Corporation, which sold four of these as an SD2-4 piece salt dip set. In December 1984, Summit Art Glass Company acquired this mold and began to use it. The Cambridge pieces are flared at the top as shown here; those made by Imperial and Summit are not.

23, 24. Maker uncertain. Two matching 36-ounce pinch decanters, possibly 1933, lettered in silver "Rye" and "Scotch", with differing clear glass stoppers. A red decanter of this shape has been pictured with a red stopper made by Paden City Glass Manufacturing Company; however, it cannot be proven at present that that stopper or either stopper shown here is correct. Many manufacturers made decanters similar to this one. Some varieties are: Bryce Brothers Company's #1, Cambridge's #1070, Co-Operative Flint Glass Company's Pookie, Fostoria Glass Company's #1928 and #2052, McKee Glass Company's large and small punch bottles and 3 dent decanter, and H.P. Sinclaire and Company's #11305. The stopper in Figure 23 may have been made by Cambridge or by Morgantown Glass Works.

25. #3400/136 6" four-toed bowl, fancy, or vase, shown in 1933 and 1934 catalogue pages.

26. #1236 7½" footed ivy ball, with clear stem and foot. This shape, made from 1931 to at least 1949, is known to have been offered in Carmen at some time in the period 1949-1953.

27. #1237 footed vase, with clear stem and foot. Made from 1931 to about 1956, this was offered in Carmen in 1949 or 1950.

28. #3400/38 12 ounce tumbler, 1931-about 1938. A catalogue page of about 1936-1938 offered it in Carmen.

29. #3400/38 ball shaped 80 ounce jug or, as redesignated by 1950, 3900/116 80 ounce ball jug, with clear handle. This shape was made from 1931 to about 1950; Carmen examples probably date from the 1930s.

30. #3400/119 ball shaped 12 ounce cordial decanter, 1933-about 1956, with clear handle and stopper.

31. #1341 or #3400/1341 1 ounce cordial, 1933-about 1956, originally included in the 3400 ball shaped line.

32. #3400/97 2 ounce perfume with dropper stopper, handle and stopper, handle and stopper clear. The earliest catalogue pages showing this, from 1932, show the upper end of the handle attached to the body, and call the item a cologne; a catalogue page of 1933 and one of about 1936-1938 show the handle attached to the neck, as here in Figure 32, and call it a perfume. This latter style was sold also without the drip rod on the stopper, as the #3400/96 2 ounce oil. This oil was catalogued first in 1933, and as late as 1950, some time after the perfume version evidently had been discontinued. It appears from recently published research by Julie Sferrazza that this oil was one of several items made by Morgantown glassware Guild, from Cambridge molds, for several years after Cambridge closed in 1958. According to Sferrazza, some Cambridge examples and all of those made by Morgantown have colored handles. Red, however, was not made by Morgantown in any of these Cambridge items.

33. #3011 figure stem 7" comport, cupped, 1931-about 1937, shown here with clear stem and foot. Some #3011 items were sold under the name Statuesque around 1938. See also Figure 35.

34. Mount Vernon #2 6½ ounce (per catalogue) tall sherbet, 1931-about 1958. Probably all Carmen pieces in this pattern were made in the 1930s. See also Figures 51-53.

35. #3011/13 1 ounce brandy, made from 1934 to 1949 and perhaps to 1956, with clear stem and foot. By the end of this period this was catalogued as a cordial, though it had originally appeared as a brandy along with a #3011/14 cordial of different bowl shape. See also Figure 33.

36. #1066 3 ounce low cocktail, 3½" tall, 1931-1934 and probably to 1940, with clear stem and foot.

37. #1066 7 ounce tall sherbet, 1931-about 1958, with clear stem and foot. In the Cambridge catalogue of about 1956, #1066 stemware has also the name Aurora.

38. Gadroon #3500/15 individual sugar and cream set, 1933-about 1956.

39. #3400/90 2-handled 2-compartment relish, made from 1931 to about 1956. Cambridge catalogues described this first as 8", once as 7½", and last as 6". It is known in Carmen with a silver deposit decoration of unknown origin.

40. Four items of Rose Point stemware of the type having feet pressed in the Rose Point design and plain bowls. This stemware was mentioned in a trade journal for February, 1935, and it apparently was then a new line. It is scarce, and may have been made for only a short time. This is in marked contrast to the long popularity of Cambridge's Rose Point etching, of similar design, introduced about the same time.

41-43, 45-50. Pieces of Tally-Ho line: (41) 1402/77 13" footed punch bowl, 1932-about 1938. The shapes in Figures 42, 43 and 45 (cup only) were offered with this style of bowl.

(42) #1402/140 5 ounce cup, clear with Carmen handle. This style of cup appears on a Cambridge catalogue page from the period 1938-1948.

(43) #1402/78 6 ounce punch mug or cup, 1933-about 1938.

(45) #1402/19 cup and saucer, 1932-about 1938. The cup was also catalogued without the saucer, as #1402/78 footed punch cup.

(46) #1402/36 14 ounce handled stein, 1932-1933, with clear handle.

(47) #1402/76 5" candlestick, 1932-about 1938.

(48) #1402/33 sugar and cream, 1932-about 1938.

(49) #1402/23 8" salad plate, 1932.

(50) #1402/3 12 ounce (10 ounce per catalogue) goblet, made from 1932 to about 1938 and probably on into the 1940s. It is reported that the 1940 Cambridge catalogue offered this item in Carmen; likely it had been made in this color for several years.

44. Candlestick made by Farber Brothers of New York City, chromium-plated metal with a red glass insert said to have come from Cambridge Glass Company. A pair of these candlesticks was #5668 in Farber Brothers' 1941 catalogue. The stem apparently was copied from the well-known Cambridge nude stem in glass (Figures 33 and 35). Farber Brothers bought many inserts from Cambridge, but also bought inserts from other manufacturers. This insert is found in several colors in Farber Brothers candlesticks and candelabras of various designs.

51-53. Mount Vernon pattern. See also Figure 34.

(51) #84 14 ounce stein, 1932-1933.

(52) #22 3 ounce footed tumbler, 1932-about 1956.

(53) #1 10 ounce goblet, 1931-about 1958.

Figures 54-58, 60-63, 65: **Duncan and Miller Glass Company,** Washington, Pennsylvania.

This firm had a long-standing reputation for fine-quality pressed glass by the time red became popular. Duncan's deep red, called simply ruby, is reported to have been introduced in 1931. It was being advertised the following year, and continued at least through 1935. According to Weatherman, it was made through the 1940s. Ruby was mentioned in Duncan advertisements in 1949 and 1950; once in 1950 it was called Royal Ruby. Duncan's 1951 price list offered ruby. Some Duncan items were continued by the United States Glass Company and its successors at Tiffin, Ohio, after Duncan and Miller Glass Company closed in 1955, but there seems to be no evidence that any of the Tiffin examples were ruby except some swans.

For another Duncan item, see Figure 243.

54. #113 Radiance 14" plate, advertised in 1937 and later and offered in ruby in Duncan's 1951 price list.

55. #115 Canterbury 8" 3-handled 3-compartment candy box and cover. Duncan and Miller was making this item by 1942. It was made later at Tiffin, Ohio, first by the United States Glass Company, and as late as 1966 by Tiffin Art Glass Corporation.

In red, this piece was offered by Duncan in the 1951 price list and reportedly in a late 1940s advertisement.

56. #121 Swirl 14" cornucopia vase. This was made in three shapes, numbered 1, 2, and 3, differing in the position into which the tail was tooled. All three varieties were available in 1943. In 1951 only the #2 shape was offered, in ruby as well as clear. The same shape in clear was being made by the United States Glass Company about 1957, as #121-117.

57. Cigarette jar lacking cover. When complete, this is in the shape of a ship's lantern. It was first made about 1936, as part of Duncan's #114 Nautical line. In 1943 it was included in Sanibel, #130 pattern, while the Nautical line as such was not in Duncan's catalogue. It is not known whether the ruby cigarette jars were sold as Nautical, as Sanibel, or neither. The base as shown here has been found with a metal cover, evidently designed especially for it; this raises the possibility that the red bases may have been made only for the firm which made the metal lid, so perhaps no ruby lid exists.

58, 60, 61, 63, 65. Pall Mall #30½ swans in four of the five sizes made. All five sizes were made by Duncan from 1943 or earlier, and were available in ruby with crystal neck in 1951. All sizes except the 7½" were offered in "Crystal, Green and Ruby" by the United States Glass Company about 1957. No production in ruby after that is known. Reportedly, swans of this shape were made at Tiffin, Ohio, as late as 1969, when the factory was known as Tiffin Glass Co.

(58) 13½", numbered 30-83 by United States Glass Company.

(60) 7½", in production by 1942. This and the size listed by Duncan as 7" apparently were made from the same mold for the body, different finishing after pressing producing a deeper shape in the length shown here. The longer of these two varieties was one of three sizes available from the Tiffin, Ohio, factory in 1966.

(61) 5½", designated 30-80 by United States Glass and by its successor, Tiffin Art Glass Corporation, which was offering this size in 1966.

(63 and 65) 12", number 30-82 by the United

States Glass Company and later by Tiffin Art Glass Corporation, which offered this size also in 1966. The rare swans combining milk-white with red as in Figure 63 were developed probably in 1949 for 1950 selling. In March of 1950, Duncan and Miller advertised in a trade journal "Announcing . . . Milk Glass that is MODERN . . . PLAIN . . .OR IN COMBINATION WITH GREEN OR ROYAL RUBY." One of the items pictured was a swan of this style, size not stated, in milk with green neck and head.

59. Swan, 9". Swans of this shape were made in a smaller size, probably in ruby by Gundersen-Pairpoint Glass Works Division of National Pairpoint Company, New Bedford, Massachusetts, about 1953. Evidently they were also made by an earlier firm at the same factory, probably by Gundersen Glass Works (1939-1952). It was reported in 1979 that the same shape had been made by Pairpoint Glass Company of Sagamore, Massachusetts, which had operated from 1970 on. All three of these firms are credited with ruby; Gundersen-Pairpoint Glass Works advertised ruby in 1953 and reportedly 1954.

62. 8 ounce mug or glass with stuck handle. This appeared as a 4 ounce size for cocktails in a 1934 Duncan advertisement. The item there was referred to as #54; the size shown here may have carried the same pattern number.

64. Two Viking Glass Company items, each 6¼": left, swan-neck candlestick; right, #974/1S dish with swan handle or bon bon with swan handle. Both were advertised in 1950, when an advertisement picturing these and other items mentioned ruby among Viking's colors. The bon bon appears also on a Viking catalogue page with a piece of the Princess pattern, said to have been introduced in 1952.

Figures 66-125: **Fenton Art Glass Company,** Williamstown, West Virginia, except as noted.

Fenton began making glass in 1907. For most, if not all, of the years since, colored glass has been its principal output.

Fenton's earliest known production of ruby

occurred in 1914. The company's inventory at the end of that year noted five items in stock in ruby (see list below). These merit special attention, not only because of being at the beginning of Fenton's large and long production of ruby glass, but because Fenton, using a selenium formula, appears to have been the first to market a line of pressed ruby glass. The two vases listed at that time have since been given names. For #509 Knotted Beads, see Figure 94; #510 Rustic reportedly has also been found in red. Both are pressed ware. A blown pitcher and pressed tumbler, both in the Fenton Drapery pattern, have been found in selenium ruby with enamel decoration (Heacock, Fenton Second, p. 63), and may be from 1914. There seems to have been some difficulty—not limited to the earliest years—in reheating pieces to develop a solid ruby color through the entire piece. Notice, for example, the yellow rim of Figure 94. Thus, Fenton's earliest effort to market ruby may have been referred to by an English trade journal in April, 1914, which spoke of Fenton's "new rose tinted glass having an amber edge, which is supplied in dishes, plates, nappies, vases and bon-bons." Heacock pictures two pieces possibly from this period which are partly red, but predominantly yellow. Whether they were heated so as to produce this coloring intentionally or accidentally is unknown. These were pressed in the Fenton Orange Tree and Grape and Cable patterns, better known in carnival glass.

Fenton was an important manufacturer of both carnival glass and stretch glass, and is credited with most of the old red pieces of each. However, each of these types of iridescent glass is scarce in red. Carnival glass was made at this factory from 1907 to about 1930, but it is difficult to determine just when the few red examples were made. Stretch glass was made here as early as 1917 and as late as 1933, but the 1924 inventory is the only one to record iridescent ruby. The items listed were plain ones, typical of those found in stretch glass. Fenton advertised these as Florentine Ruby.

It appears that before 1920 Fenton made only rather small quantities of ruby, but by 1925 this had changed. A company catalogue from the early 1920s contains the following:

"Ruby, the idea has long prevailed that only from Bohemia or Venice could be obtained this exceptionally rich color, the despair of the ordinary glass worker.

"We have succeeded in producing a ruby that for richness, depth of color, and fire will compare favorably with the best product of the famous old world glass makers.

"Our color is not stained, painted or cased, it is in the glass, ruby all the way through."

Inventories for the years 1926-1930 are not detailed enough to provide a clear picture. A substantial amount of ruby was in stock at the end of 1931, and the color remained strong through 1938.

One example has been found of a vase apparently made at this time in selenium ruby cased over milk-white.

Published here for the first time are lists of ruby items in stock at the Fenton Art Glass company. These were copied from the Company's inventories taken at the end of each year from 1914—the first mention of ruby—through 1942. (The original inventories are dated either December 31 or January 1 of the following year. For example, what is referred to here as the 1914 inventory is actually dated January 1, 1915.) The 1916 inventory record does not survive; other years are omitted because there is no mention of ruby.

While all of the items specified as ruby are included here, these lists must not be understood as including every ruby item made at Fenton during any year. It is not to be expected that every different item would be on hand at the time the inventory was taken. Also, the colors of the items listed were not always specified; notably the 1928 inventory makes no mention, and the 1922, 1923, 1929, and 1930 inventories make very few mentions, of colors, although most of the items on hand were probably in color.

Despite such shortcomings, these lists will be found useful as a source of reliable dates for particular items, as well as other information. Because it is not possible to picture in this book every item inventoried, references to Fenton Glass The First Twenty-Five Years 1907-1932 and Fenton Glass The Second Twenty-Five Years, both by William Heacock have been added to make items listed easier to identify.

In the original inventories, ditto marks were often used to indicate that a word was to be repeated from a line above; the word indicated appears here in place of the ditto marks. Otherwise, the abbreviations, spelling, and punctuation of the

originals have been preserved. In this way the reader has the opportunity to examine the evidence and draw his own conclusions, rather than see only those of the writer.

The way items were valued for inventory was not always the same. According to Dr. Eugene C. Murdock, from 1907 to 1921 the firm's financial records were kept by Thomas P. Butcher, "not a trained or systematic bookkeeper . . . About the time of Butcher's death in 1921, a certified public accountant was brought in, and a new bookkeeping system was instituted, marking an end to the earlier chaos." Frank M. Fenton says "From studying the records, it appears to me that, up through 1921, we were using wholesale prices to price the inventory. About 1922 we began to change. When the Florentine line was sold, some of it was priced at retail . . . About 1925, the method of pricing stabilized at retail." Mr. Fenton further notes the discounts which were then figured from these retail prices. Up through 1930, these discounts were usually deducted from inventory totals, so that the entries printed here are at retail. 1924 may be an exception to this. After 1930, the entries which you see here evidently reflect a 50% discount from retail.

After 1942, ruby seems to have made only two minor appearances in the Fenton line before 1966. First, three sizes of Georgian pattern tumblers were offered in ruby for short periods between July 1, 1952, and July 1, 1954, and possibly a little later. Then in 1962 and 1963, Fenton offered a few blown items in what the company called Plated Amberina, a cased glass consisting of an outer layer of selenium ruby over an inner layer of milk-white. This did not exactly duplicate the older glass known as Plated Amberina, which was made about 1886 by the New England Glass Works.

In 1966 Fenton offered the Hobnail slipper (Figure 82), seven pieces of the Thumbprint pattern (Figure 71), and three other items, in ruby. Thus began another period of extensive ruby production, which continues to the present. This has included a revival of red carnival glass.

During many years Fenton has made also blown items in what it called Ruby Overlay. This is the color commonly called cranberry, a cased glass of crystal with gold ruby; it is not the selenium ruby of the items discussed above, with which this book is primarily concerned. Fenton has used gold ruby in various combinations, for example, Ruby Snowcrest, which has a rim of milk-white.

About July, 1952, Fenton revised its system of numbering its products; since then, each item has had its own four-digit number.

In recent years the Fenton line has carried a trademark molded into the glass. An oval enclosing the name Fenton was the first design. It seems to have been used to some extent in 1969, though the January 1980 Catalog Supplement states: "Beginning in 1970 we began marking Fenton items with the [illustration] trademark. For the collectors to distinguish production of the 'seventies' from the 'eighties', all production after January 1, 1980 will show the Fenton logo with an 8 added to it - [illustration showing an 8 under the word Fenton, within the oval]". For some items about 1983, and for all new items of 1985 and

thereafter, Fenton introduced a new trademark using a distinctive style of F rather than the full word Fenton. This did not immediately end use of the older mark, but was to appear on new products as they would be introduced.

For more Fenton items, see Figures 473, 606, 608-612, 614-616, 619, 629, and 636.

66. #8238 Persian Medallion basket, 7½". This was made, apparently in amethyst carnival, by about 1974, and was in the Fenton line for 1977 in Ruby Iridescent and other colors, but was not shown in that year's catalogue in ruby without an iridescent finish. The handles on these carnival examples are not reeded, as this one is. This pattern was made by Fenton as early as about 1911, but apparently not in basket form before the 1970s. Apparently the name Persian Medallion (sometimes Persian Medallions) was first applied by Marion Hartung in 1960, and later adopted by the manufacturer. Fenton is not known to have used a name for this pattern in earlier years.

67. #9166 48 ounce pitcher, made in ruby in 1981. This pitcher in other colors, with several matching items, was sold in 1961 under the pattern name Jacqueline. In the 1970s a sample of the pitcher was made in Fenton's Burmese color.

This design appears to have been copied from a pattern made from 1890 to 1896, by Fostoria Shade and Lamp Company, Fostoria, Ohio, and its successor, Consolidated Lamp and Glass Company, first at Fostoria and then at Coraopolis, Pennsylvania. This pattern may have been named Rose by its makers then; it has since been called Pink Rose and Rose Petals. Apparently the only items made in the 1890s were night lamps and a sugar shaker, neither of which has been made by Fenton, and a salt shaker, of different shape from Fenton's. The Victorian pieces are not known in ruby.

68. #9137 Fine Cut and Block basket, 6½" (7" per catalogues, 7" high per January 1985 Price List). This item was first made, evidently beginning in 1973 or earlier, in the Olde Virginia Glass line, which was made by Fenton but not sold under the Fenton name. It appeared in the Fenton line 1980-1986, in ruby 1982-1984. This example was bought at the Fenton factory. In 1989 it reappeared, in Teal Marigold iridescent glass, but with a double crimp in the rim, rather than the style of crimp shown here. Its number remained 9137.

Fine Cut and Block was originally the unnamed #25 pattern of King Glass Company, Pittsburgh, made from 1886-1891. King did not make it in red, nor, as far as is known, in either of the shapes shown here (Figures 68 and 81). The name Fine Cut and Block was used by author Ruth Webb Lee, and thus was accepted by collectors before Fenton adopted both the design and the name.

69. #3734 Hobnail basket, 11½", made from 1959 on, in ruby in 1977-1980. Fenton catalogues describe this as 12", which the January 1985 Price List gives as the height; Fenton's 1989 catalogue and January 1989 Order Blank describe it as 10½" high.

Fenton has made hobnail items since the 1930s, but many others used the Hobnail motif before Fenton. It can be dated back as far as 1886, and was very popular in the next few years, when it was often called Dew Drop. It was not then made in the ruby color shown here, though some was made in gold ruby (cranberry). Various manufacturers took up the design again around 1930. About 1931-1940 the name Hobnail, used in the writings of Ruth Webb Lee, became generally accepted by collectors and manufacturers. Most of Fenton's

Hobnail shapes, including the three here (Figures 69, 80, and 82) seem to have been originated by Fenton. For other red Hobnail items, see Figures 196, 197, 240, 440, 568, and 594.

70 and 72. #7333 heart relish in (70) ruby with milk crest and (72) milk with ruby crest. Fenton's January, 1985, Price List gives an 8" measurement for this item. While it was in the Fenton line 1955-1986 and was marketed through others in 1988, the color combinations shown here seem to have been offered only briefly, in 1979.

71. Basket, 6³/₄". This is evidently the Thumbprint "#4434 . . . 7" Basket" which is reported to have been in the Fenton line in 1969 and 1970 in other colors. No illustration of that basket could be found, but the one shown here appears similar to the #4438 Thumbprint 8¹/₂" basket which Fenton offered in ruby from 1966 through 1980.

This is another case in which Fenton copied an old design not originally made in this shape or color. Thumbprint was made by several factories in the Pittsburgh area and in Wheeling, as early as around 1875. The name Thumbprint was not used by the manufacturers then, but it has been used at least since the 1930s by collectors. Fenton was using this name by 1962.

73. #8361 bell, Barred Oval, 6" high per catalogues, introduced in 1985 and offered through 1988, in ruby all four years.

This design was copied from the United States Glass Company's #15004 tableware pattern, first made in 1891 in Pittsburgh. United States Glass did not make it in the shapes shown here (Figures 73, 74, and 79), or in red glass, though some pieces were stained red on certain portions. The name Barred Oval, now used by Fenton, was given by Ruth Webb Lee in 1944.

74. #8372 candleholder, Barred Oval, 6" high, put into the Fenton line for 1985 and discontinued at the end of 1987.

75. #1939 Daisy and Button oval basket, made by Fenton in 1965 and 1966 (and possibly longer), discontinued, and made again 1981-1984; ruby was offered 1982-1984. Although Fenton called this Daisy and Button, its pattern is not exactly the one which Fenton has called by that name in other items, and which is known to collectors of Victorian pressed glass as Daisy and Button. Rather, this is a reproduction of a piece in the pattern known as Lady Chippendale, which was registered in Great Britain in 1891 and reportedly was made by George Davidson and Company, Gateshead-on-Tyne, England. This piece is not known to have been made in red other than by Fenton.

76. Mini-basket in "Ruby with snowcrest petticoat and handle," as described by Charles and Zeta Todd of Aurora, Colorado. This is one of 375 in this color combination made by Fenton for the Todds, who advertised them for sale in 1985 and 1986. The same item was also made in four other colors for the Todds. It had been in the Fenton line in 1942 as the #37 2¹/₂" miniature basket, fan (shaped). Todds advertised theirs, which were made in colors not used in 1942, 4" and as 4¹/₂" high.

77. #1700 fairy light, made as early as 1972 and still being made in 1989, apparently always with base in clear and shade in ruby, and usually decorated. What appears to be the same item is #7300, 1972-present, in Fenton catalogues where the shade is in nearly opaque colors; probably it does not have the diamond optic in the shade which #1700 has. With the opalescent Spiral design in the shade, the same shape is #3100, offered in Fenton's 1979-1980 catalogue. Fenton had used the number 1700 for a tableware pattern many years earlier (Figures 117-123, 125).

78. #1760 petite bell, 4¹/₂", made in ruby 1982-present, also made in various other colors, and often decorated.

79. #8333 small basket, Barred Oval, 6", a shape introduced at the beginning of 1985 and discontinued at the end of 1987, both in ruby.

80. #3667 Hobnail bell, 5¹/₂" high, in the Fenton January, 1985, Price List. This shape was being made by 1969. To at least 1971 the ridges on the handles were finely notched; in the 1977-78 catalogue, these ridges were smooth. This item in ruby was discontinued at the end of 1984; it was discontinued entirely at the end of 1986.

81. #9144 ringholder, Fine Cut and Block. This item has been in the Fenton line from January, 1982 to the present. It has appeared in Fenton's catalogues in several other colors, but the exact date of ruby is uncertain.

82. #3995 slipper, Hobnail, 5" made from 1941 to the present. In ruby, it has been in the Fenton Line 1966-1979 and again from June, 1987 to the present. Until about July, 1952, this and many other Fenton Hobnail shapes shared the pattern number 389. By 1949, most of these shapes were individually identified by added numbers, this slipper being 389-3995. The 389 designation was dropped in 1952.

83. #1621 10" oval bowl. Smaller dishes of matching design were #1621 bon bons in a Fenton catalogue and in Fenton's 1928 and 1929 inventories. They are listed with the #1703 cutting in 1929. The larger size of Figure 83 appears in only one inventory entry, in 1936: "10 doz. 1621-10" bowls asstd". However, this size is also known with the #1703 cutting, suggesting that it too was being made about 1929. It is not known if ruby examples of either size were ever cut.

84. Probably a Cambridge Glass Company Carmen color hat, made at an undetermined date in the period 1931-1958. Fenton made hats of similar shape, in several sizes and various colors, beginning in 1937 (see Figure 613).

85. #175 8½" Leaf Plate. This appears in Fenton inventories for 1935 through 1938, 1941, and 1942, in ruby in 1936. The same item was made as #5116 from 1955 to at least 1966, but it does not seem to have been made in ruby in the latter period.

86. 8" plate, maker uncertain. This appears to match Fenton's #1502 Diamond Optic line (Figures 87 and 93). The company's 1929 inventory lists #1502 8" plates in both round and octagon shapes, but no picture of the round one could be found. It may have been on hand at the other inventories from 1927 through 1931, but the records fail to specify the shape. None of these entries mention ruby. Other manufacturers, notably A.H. Heisey and Company of Newark, Ohio, made pieces of similar pattern. In fact, Heisey made an 8" round

plate, but it appears to differ from this one in the number of diamonds, and Heisey made very little red glass.

87. #1502 Diamond Optic 10" cupped bowl. Fenton's 1927 and 1928 inventories list #1502 10" shallow cupped bowls, evidently the same as this one, and the 1929 inventory includes "1502-10" Nappies (Bowls)". None of these entries specify colors.

88. 8½" fan vase, maker unknown, probably 1925 or later.

89. #1620 sherbet, recorded by inventories for the years 1933 through 1939, in ruby each year except 1937. The #1620 pattern, which Fenton reportedly named Plymouth, was made in various bar and table items.

90. Fenton candlestick, 3", possibly #1623. This shape may be found with either flowers, as shown here, or ribs on the underside of the foot, and, perhaps with a plain foot. Only the ribbed type can be identified in Fenton catalogue illustrations which have been reprinted; it is #1623 on catalogue pages of about 1927-1928. The base design is not visible in other catalogue illustrations, dating into the 1930s, which also use this number. Fenton inventories recorded #1623 candlesticks in 1928 through 1931, 1933, and 1937; ruby was specified in 1937 only. It appears likely that the entries in the latter years of this period refer to the type shown here. The ribbed type, which may not have been made in red, has been called Double Dolphin, Dolphin Twins, Swirled Dolphin and simply Dolphin. In 1953 Fenton used the number 1623 for a different item.

91 and 92. #1621 crimp bon bon, 7¼", and #1621 square bon bon, 5¼". This was made in at least two other shapes also, though not necessarily in ruby; all four shapes are shown on a catalogue page of about 1928. #1621 bon bons appear in Fenton's inventories for 1928, 1929, 1935, and 1936; the entries are not specific as to shape, and none mention ruby.

93. #1502 Diamond Optic 7½" comport bon bon. Pieces from the same mold as this one were hand

worked into several shapes; entries in Fenton inventories indicate that some of these were made in 1929 and probably the previous two years. These entries did not specify colors.

94. #509 Knotted Beads 11" vase, one of the first items Fenton is known to have made in ruby. Fenton's 1914 inventory records is in ruby and in crystal. #509 vases of unspecified color in the 1913, 1914 and 1919 inventories were probably carnival glass.

95. Duncan and Miller Glass Company's #103 Georgian wine, 4". This is part of an extensive line of tableware, in which the figure and some of the shapes are very much like those in Fenton's pattern shown in the next item and several other items on the same page. Duncan's line was made as early as 1927, in ruby from about the beginning of 1932. Available Duncan catalogue illustrations of the wine seem to be from around 1939, though it may have been made for some years before that. Fenton's cocktail is similar in appearance, but has a broader bowl and a thicker stem.

96. #1611 Agua Caliente decanter, 21 ounce. This item appears in Fenton's inventories for 1931, when ruby was mentioned, and 1934 and 1935. See also Figures 95, 97, and 102-107.

97. This appears to be either Cambridge Glass Company's #316 Georgian sundae, 1930, or Fenton's #1611 Agua Caliente cupped sherbet, 1931-1939, which was made in ruby throughout those years. Duncan and Miller's #103 Georgian footed jello (see discussion of Figure 95) and especially Paden City Glass Manufacturing Company's #69 Georgian 4 ounce regular sherbet are also similar according to catalogue illustrations. Paden City's Georgian (also known as Aristocrat) line probably began to appear in 1934; it was made in many items, most of which are different in shape from their counterparts in Fenton's Agua Caliente, though the motif matches. Some Paden City items, including the sherbet similar to this, were made by Canton Glass Company, Marion, Indiana, after Paden City's 1951 closing. Paden City likely made their variety in ruby, and Canton may have also. Still another firm which has made a tableware line of this basic design, reportedly beginning in 1953,

is Viking Glass Company. While most of Viking's Georgian (#69 or #6900) shapes seem to be distinctive, at least two tumbler molds had been Paden City's, so perhaps the Viking sherbet so much like this one also had been. Many items in Viking's Georgian have been made in ruby up to at least 1983.

98. #848 three footed ash tray. 4", an item made 1934-1939, in ruby 1934-1937.

99. #1645 nymph figure, 6", in a 2½" flower block. The nymph figure appears in Fenton inventories for 1928 through 1934, and again in the 1939 inventory and a 1941 price list; the only years when ruby was specified were 1933 and 1934.

Collectors sometimes call this the September Morn nymph, because of its resemblance to the female figure in the painting September Morn by the French painter Paul Chabas. The flower block here was regularly used by Fenton with this figure. It may be the #1643, which is listed adjacent to the nymph figure in the 1928 and 1934 inventories, and in ruby in the latter year. One page of Fenton sales material featuring the nymph and block with the #1234 console bowl designates the nymph and the block as #1234, but the nymph was #1645 in five inventories, 1928 and 1930 through 1933.

100. #848 bowl, 9", possibly in the shape Fenton called a 9" flared console bowl, one of at least four ways this bowl was shaped in the years it was made, (about 1926-1938). Ruby examples were inventoried in 1933 and later.

101. #848 candleholder, 4", made 1932-1938; in ruby, 1933-1936.

102-107. Pieces in #1611 Agua Caliente pattern; see also Figure 472. Only a tumbler in this pattern appears in Fenton's 1930 inventory; a wide range of pieces appear in 1931 and each year through 1939, always including ruby. No #1611 items were in stock at the end of 1940. Eight shapes in the pattern were on hand at the end of 1941; a year later only goblets and tumblers, each in ruby. One Fenton catalogue page calls this "No. 1611 Georgian Tableware Line." Georgian may have been intended as a name or merely a description; it was clearly named Agua Caliente elsewhere.
(102) 54 ounce jug, ice lipped. What is apparently

Blenko

1

2

3

4

5

6

7

8

9

10

11

12

13   14   15

16   17   18

19   20   21   22

Cambridge and Others

23

24

25

26

27

28

29

30

31

32

33

34

35

36

37

38

39

Cambridge and Others

40   41   42   43   44

45   46   47   48

49   50   51   52   53

Duncan & Miller
and Other Swans

54

55

56

57

58

59

60

61

62

63

64

65

Fenton

66   67   68   69

70   71   72   73   74

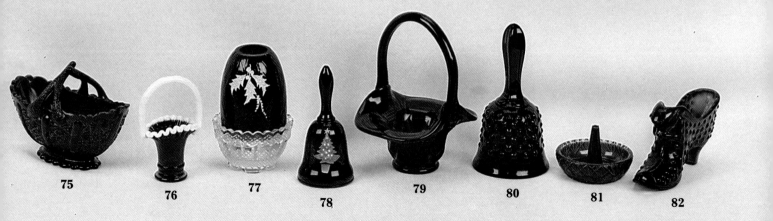

75   76   77   78   79   80   81   82

Fenton and Others

83

84

85

86

87

88

89

90

91

92

93

94
95
96
97
98
99
100
101
102
103
104
105
106
107
108
109
110
111

112   113   114   115   116

117   118   119   120   121   122

123   124   125

Fostoria and Others

126   127   128   129   130

131   132   133   134

135   136   137   138

139

140

141

142

143

144

145

146

147

148

149

150

Anchor Hocking

151

152

153

154

155

156

157

158

159

160

161

162

163   164   165   165A   166   167

168   169   170A

170

171   172   173   174

Anchor Hocking

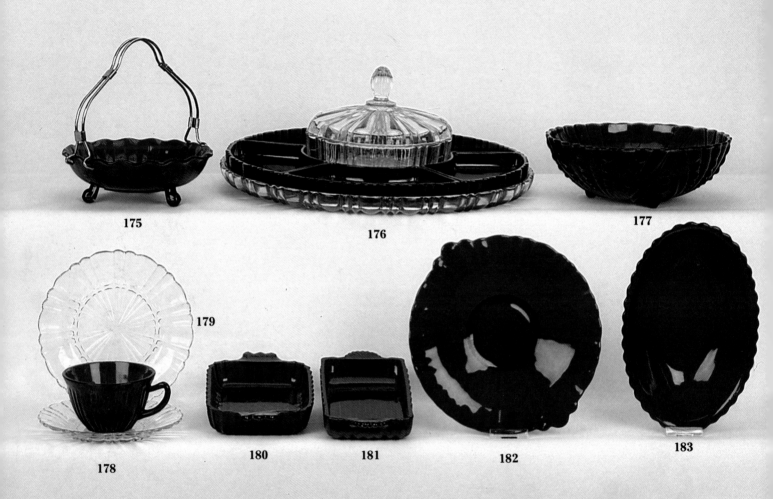

175

176

177

179

178 180 181 182 183

184 185 186 187 188 189

190   191   192   193   194   195

196   197   198   199   200   201

202   203   204   205   206   207

Anchor Hocking

208   209   210   211

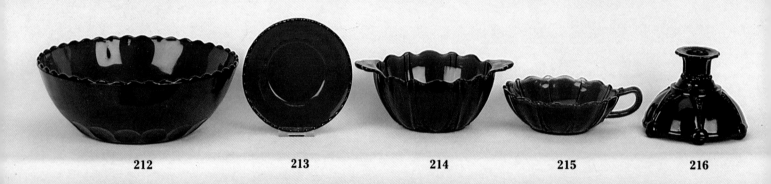

212   213   214   215   216

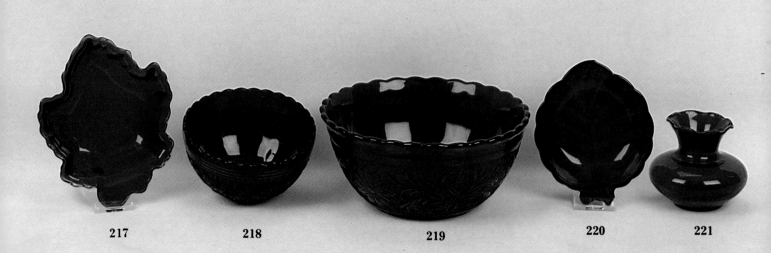

217   218   219   220   221

Anchor Hocking

222 223 224 225 226 227

228 229 230 231 232

233 234 235 236 237

Imperial and Others

238   239   240   241   242

243   244   245   246   247

248   249   250   251   252

253

254

255

256

257

258

259

260

261

262

263

264

265

266

267

268
269
270
271
272
273
274
275
276
277
278
279
280
281

282

283

284   285   286   287   288

289   290   291

Macbeth-Evans and McKee

292

293

294

295

296

297

298

299

300

301

302

303

304

305

38

306   307   308   309   310   311

312   313   314   315

316   317   318   319   320   321

New Martinsville
and Others

322   323   324   325

326   327   328   329   330

331   332   333   334

335

336

337

338

339

340

341

342

343

344

345

346

347

348

349

350

351

352

353

354

355

356

357

358

359

Miscellany

360

361

362

363

364

365

366

367

368

369

370

371   372   373   374

375   376   377   378   379   380

384

381   382   383   385   386   387

Miscellany

388

389

390

391

392

393

394

395

396

397

398

399

400

401

402

403

404

405

406

407

408

409   410   411

412   413   414

415   416   417

Paden City

418

419

420

421

422

423

424

425

426

427

428

Miscellany

429   430   431   432   433   434

435   436   437   438   439

440   441   442   443   444   445   446

Miscellany

447

447A

448

448A

449

449A

450

451

450A

452

453

453A

454

455A
50

455

456

456A

457

458A

458

Miscellany

459

460

461

462

463

464

465

466

467

468

468A

469

468B

Miscellany

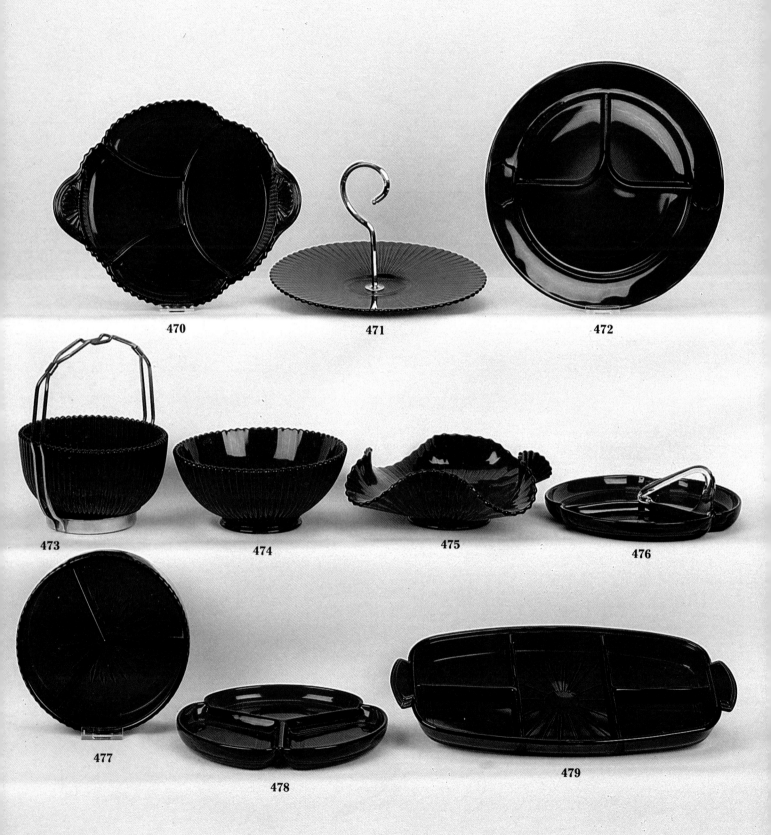

470

471

472

473

474

475

476

477

478

479

Miscellany

480

481

482

483

484

485

Anchor Hocking

487

486

487A

488

Miscellany

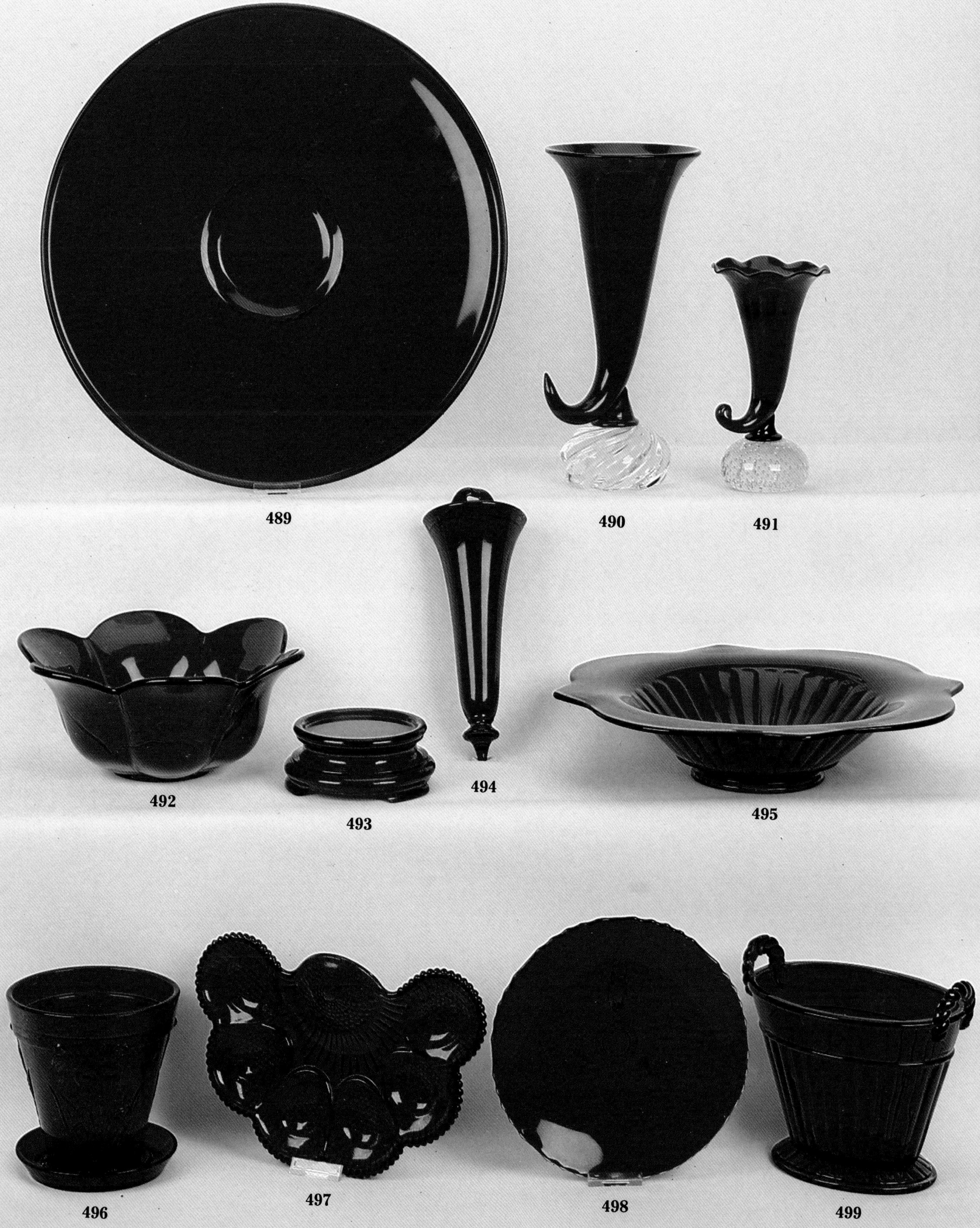

489 490 491

492 493 494 495

496 497 498 499

Miscellany

500

501

502

503

504

505

506

507

508

508A

509

510   511   511A   511B   511C

Miscellany

512   513A   513   514A   514

515   516   517   518   519   520

521   522   523   524   525

Venetion Glass

526

527

528

529

530

531

532

533

534

535

536

537

538

539

Viking Glass

540   541   542   543   544   545   546   547   548

549   550   551   552   553   554   555

556   557   558   559   560   561

Westmoreland

562

563

564

565

566

567

568

569

570

571

572

573

574

575

576

577

578

579

580

581

582

583

584

585

586

587

588

589

590

591

592

593

594

594A

595

596

597

598

599

600

601

602

603

Fenton and Others

604

605

606

607

608

609

610

611

612

613

614

615

63

Miscellany

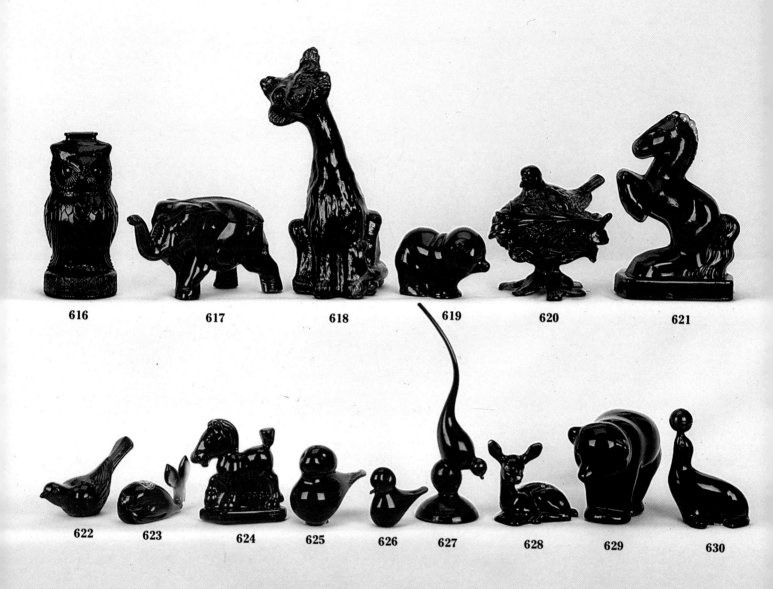

616   617   618   619   620   621

622   623   624   625   626   627   628   629   630

631   632   633   634   635   636   637   638   639

the same #1611 jug was described as ½ gallon by Fenton in another place. This jug was made both with and without an ice lip. The ice lipped variety was specified in only one inventory, that of 1932; it was listed in ruby. The jug appears without mention of the ice lip in several following years, as late as 1939, and was on hand in ruby each time. Duncan Miller's #103 Georgian ½ gallon jug is very similar in shape and pattern. The Duncan jug was made from 1928 to the late 1930's, probably in ruby for some of that time (see discussion of Figure 95).

(103) Sugar and cream set, which appears in Fenton's inventories 1931-1939, in ruby each year except 1935.

(104) High sherbet, 6 ounce, 1931-1941; this was inventoried in ruby in 1931, 1941, and five of the years between. It is another item very similar to one by Duncan Miller, the #103 Georgian 6 ounce footed ice cream or saucer champagne.

(105) Goblet, 10 ounce, listed in each Fenton inventory from 1931 through 1939 and agin in 1941 and 1942, being in stock in ruby each year. Here again is a Fenton item very much like one in Duncan Miller's #103 Georgian pattern, described as a 9 ounce goblet.

(106) Salt pepper shaker with apparently original metal top, 4½" tall, inventoried in 1932, 1933, and 1935 through 1939, in ruby each year.

(107) 8" salad plate, inventoried in 1931-1939 and 1941, ruby being specified each year except 1932 and 1939. Each of the three rows of figures around Fenton's salad plate contains 20 segments. The similar 7½" and 8½" (catalogue sizes) Duncan and Miller Georgian plates appear to have 24 in each row.

108-111. Items in the Fenton's Basket pattern.

(108 and 111) #1092 crimped bowl and plate bon bon. Various shapes from the #1092 mold (apparently there was only one) appear in scattered years' inventories as early as 1911; ruby is not mentioned, but examples likely date from around 1935 and 1936, the last two years #1092 was listed. Fenton's #8222 Basket Weave bowl, made in many colors from about 1970 to 1984, and the #8323 bowl and #8335 basket introduced more recently, may be from the same mold.

(109) #1093 8¾" crimp fancy nappy. The mold for

this item was evidently made about the end of 1919. Various shapes made from it were inventoried in the 1921-1926 period and from 1933 through 1936; only in 1936 was ruby mentioned. At least some of the ruby examples in this shape, as well as some other shapes and colors, were sold to the S.S. Kresge Company.

(110) #1091 crimped candle stick. This item does not appear in any reprint of a Fenton catalogue or advertisement, but is listed in inventories for 1936 and 1938, described in the latter year as crimped; ruby ones were in stock in 1936.

112. New Martinsville Glass Manufacturing Company's #18 Crystal Eagle salt or pepper (top probably not original), 4½", 1936-1937. This was among the Crystal Eagle items advertised in February, 1936, as available in ruby. See Figures 400-402 for more of this pattern.

113-115. Three shapes of the #1800 Sheffield 6½" vase, which was entered in ruby and other colors in the 1937 Fenton inventory.

(113) Flared cupped.

(114) Crimped, 6¼" per catalogue.

(115) Flared, 6¼" per catalogue.

116. #1681 10½" basket, which appeared in inventory records first in 1931, and last in 1938, and was noted in ruby in 1933.

117-122 and 125. #1700 Lincoln Inn pieces. Fenton's inventory first showed Lincoln Inn on hand at the end of 1928; probably it was a new line for 1929. It continued to be on hand each year through 1939, but after 1932 the only ruby #1700 mentioned was one item in 1933 and one in 1938. Fenton has used the number 1700 in recent years for an unrelated item (Figure 77).

(117) Cup, 1928-about 1940, inventoried in ruby 1931.

(118) Finger bowl, 4¾", on the saucer which should be under the cup in Figure 117. The finger bowl was inventoried in 1930 without color specified, and in 1937-1939 in crystal. The saucer, made from 1928 to about 1940, was inventoried in ruby in 1931.

(119) 8" plate, made 1928-1940, exact date of ruby

unknown. Presumably some of the #1700 8" plates inventoried were a variant with an intaglio fruit design pressed in the center and usually frosted on crystal. This type was evidently first made about 1935, when it was pictured in a Fenton advertisement, and some plates began to be noted in inventories as satin finished.

(120) Sherbet, 4", made 1928-1939, in ruby in 1931. This shape is pictured as a sherbet in two different Fenton catalogues, and was pictured in a 1928 advertisement. The dates after 1928 are from inventories which list sherbets with no further shape or size description, and are assumed to refer to this style; however, a 4½" cone-shaped sherbet is also reported to have been found.

(121) A Fenton catalogue pictures this item with the caption "Wine or Cocktail." No other style of wine or of cocktail in #1700 is known to exist, yet four of Fenton's inventories—1929-1931, 1935, and 1937—list wines and cocktails separately. Therefore, it is unclear which inventory entries refer to the shape shown here. In addition to those just mentioned, the 1932 and 1933 inventories list cocktails. Wines were recorded in ruby in 1931, cocktails in 1931 and 1932.

(122) Goblet, 9 ounce, 1928-1939, inventoried in ruby in 1931.

(125) Sugar and cream in one of two styles made in this pattern. These have a higher foot than the other style. Both types were pictured in Fenton catalogues, apparently at different dates. The type shown here is evidently the earlier, as it was pictured in a 1928 advertisement, whereas the other was included in a wholesaler's 1940 catalogue. Inventories did not distinguish between them, but simply listed sugars and creams, beginning in 1928 and ending in 1939, noting ruby in 1931. It is not known if the lower-footed type was made in ruby.

123 and 124. Two 3-footed bowls in the same pattern, 123 crimped and 124 flared, apparently made by Fenton, possibly in 1932. Two other items in this pattern are documented as Fenton's. One is the #1933 tumbler, which appears in the inventories of 1932 through 1935 and 1937, in ruby in 1934 and 1935. The other item matching, though given a different number by Fenton, is the #107 vase, inventoried in 1932, 1933, and 1934, in ruby in the first and last years. These bowls do not appear in any reprint of a Fenton catalogue or advertisement, so their pattern number is uncertain. The tumbler and vase just discussed were the only items of #1933 and #107 inventoried, except for one puzzling entry in 1932: "1933-1235-5" Nap - Green & Rose". The pieces in Figures 123 and 124 could be #1933 nappies, if the 5" figure was meant to apply only to those in #1235, which have not been identified.

Figures 126-134, 139-150: **Fostoria Glass Company,** Moundsville, West Virginia

By the mid-1930s, this company was one of the largest producers of handmade glassware in the United States. In October, 1934, Fostoria advertised to the public a line of stemware, "Westchester, Fostoria's newest pattern," stating that it came "in crystal, in colors including Fostoria's gorgeous new Oriental Ruby and in combinations of color and crystal." According to Hazel Marie Weatherman, ruby was first included in a company catalogue in 1935. The term "Oriental Ruby" may have been short-lived. A Fostoria price list dated July 1, 1935 used simply "Ruby" in listing the more than 130 items available in this color. The principal group in any one pressed pattern was 17 serving items in #2510 Sun-Ray (Figure 139). Two full lines of blown stemware—#6011 Neo Classic and #6012 Westchester and six items in #6013 were available with ruby bowls. Weatherman states that Fostoria continued to offer ruby through 1941.

Fostoria's next production of ruby, as far as the present writer can learn, was in 1961. A July 15, 1961, price list offered ten items in the Crown Collection (Figures 127, 133) in ruby, and seven items of #6080 Fascination stemware with blown ruby bowls. Also, one item was available in "Ruby Mist;" it may be ruby glass frosted by the use of acid.

28 items comprised the list of ruby for the beginning of 1962. The numbers of different items offered in ruby in Fostoria's catalogues of some of the following years were: 1965—59 items; 1967—50; 1971—41; January 1, 1974— 35; 1974-1975 (November 1, 1974)—35; 1975- 1976 (November 1, 1975)—35; January 1, 1982 price list—38.

At various times in the period 1965-1982,

certain nineteenth-century style items appeared in Fostoria's catalogues as the "Henry Ford Museum Collection," and others carried the caption "By Special Arrangement with the Henry Ford Museum." These were made in various colors, including ruby, throughout this period for the items with the latter notation. Pieces from both groups are found embossed with the letters "HFM," apparently to indicate that they are copies (in some cases adaptations) of pieces in the collection of The Henry Ford Museum, Dearborn, Michigan.

In Early 1982, Fostoria introduced five pieces of its famous American pattern in ruby (Figures 129, 130). While American had been in production for many years, chiefly in clear glass, none is known to have been marketed in ruby before 1982.

By this time, some Fostoria items were being made by machinery alongside the workmen making others by the hand methods long associated with the Fostoria name. During 1982, all pressing and blowing of glass by hand in the Moundsville factory was stopped in favor of machine processes. A letter from the company announcing this to all Fostoria dealers was dated May 19, 1982. This letter said that the change was "due to the overwhelming acceptance of our entire line of lead crystal products and casual stemware which is contrasted by the constantly rising cost of maintaining the handblown and handmolded glassware."

After this, the Fostoria Glass Company began to have some items made for it by other firms. Thus, while the cessation of hand glassmaking meant the end of production of ruby glass in this factory, it did not permanently eliminate ruby from the Fostoria line. Fostoria continued to offer ruby, but in the American pattern only. These same five pieces were made for Fostoria by Viking Glass Company, of New Martins-ville, West Virginia, until 1986. The pieces in Figures 129 and 130 were among those available in ruby by March, 1982, so evidently these were made at Moundsville, but most others were made by Viking; all were sold as Fostoria. Viking made some Fostoria items in clear, Peach, and possibly other colors, all by hand. In the same period, L.E. Smith Glass Company, of Mt. Pleasant, Pennsylvania, made by hand some clear glass items for Fostoria; this may include pieces in the American pattern.

In December, 1983, Lancaster Colony Corporation acquired all outstanding stock of the Fostoria Glass Company. Thereafter, some Fostoria items were made by the Indiana Glass Company, Dunkirk, Indiana, another glass manufacturer owned by Lancaster Colony. These were made—some by hand, some by machine—in clear, Peach, Brown, and other colored glass.

About the end of February, 1986, glass production in the Fostoria factory at Moundsville stopped entirely.

The Fostoria name is still being used for a line of glassware. The current catalogue (undated) includes the Heritage, Transition, and Virginia patterns and a few other items formerly made at the Moundsville factory, along with more recently introduced items. The latter, and most of the items on seven loose sheets accompanying the catalogue, appear to be imported glass. The only ruby shown or mentioned is in the Virginia giftware, which Fostoria's New York sales staff advises has been discontinued.

126. #1827 Rambler pattern piece, described in an old Fostoria catalogue as "8 inch Nappy Flared to 10 inch." This pattern reportedly was made in clear glass, 1911-1915. Two other items in Rambler were made in ruby in 1970 and 1971: a #1827/211 10½" salad bowl, of different shape than shown here, and a #1827/801 9" footed vase. Probably the bowl in Figure 126 was made about these latter years.

127. #2750/386 Hapsburg Crown footed chalice and cover, 9½" high, 1961-1965. This appeared in Fostoria's 1961 and 1962 illustrated price lists simply as a numbered item in the Crown Collection (see also Figue 133), but by 1965 the Hapsburg designation had been added. All three price lists offered it in ruby.

128. Coin glass #1372/799 8" bud vase, an item made 1961-1982, in ruby 1967-1982.

129. American pattern footed bud vase, flared, 6". Fostoria offered this item from 1960, and probably earlier, to 1986. By 1960 and to at least 1975, it was numbered 2056/763; the ruby examples were made 1982-1986, and so under Fostoria's numbering system then in use were designated AM02/736. This item and the one in Figure 130 were not in Fostoria's January 1, 1982, price list, but were offered by March of that year. Red American pieces were not made at the Fostoria factory after about May, 1982, but were made for Fostoria Glass

Company by Viking Glass Company. It therefore appears that the very first examples of these items were made at Fostoria's factory in Moundsville, but most examples were made later by Viking.

130. American 10" salad bowl. Fostoria was making this shape in the American pattern from 1961, and probably earlier, to 1986. From 1961 to at least 1975 it carried the number 2056/211. The ruby examples were made 1982-1986, as AM02/211. Although sold under the Fostoria name, most ruby examples of this bowl were probably made by Viking Glass Company, as was Figure 129.

131. Coin Glass #1372/354 (or CO 05/354) candy box and cover, $4\frac{1}{8}$" high, made from 1961, and probably earlier, to 1982, in ruby 1967-1982.

132. HO 02/584 party server, 1982. There is a partition inside, not visible in this photograph. This was one of ten ruby items shown under the heading "Holly and Ruby Giftware" in Fostoria's 1982 catalogue. Some of the other items in this group carried the same pattern as this server and numbers with the same HO prefix. Although these letters must have stood for Holly, this pattern must not be confused with the Holly cutting offered by Fostoria in the same catalogue and in many earlier years.

133. #2751/195 Navarre Crown 9" bowl, shown in Fostoria's 1961, 1962, and 1965 catalogues, offered each time in ruby. While this was included in the Crown Collection in 1961 and 1962, as was Figure 127, the Navarre name was added between then and 1965.

134. Coin Glass #1372/499 handled nappy, 5". This item was made from 1961 (and probably earlier) to 1980, in ruby 1967-1975.

135. Pickle, maker uncertain, probably 1930s. Pickle dishes similar to this were made by Imperial Glass Company and its successor, Imperial Glass Corporation, about 1930-1936, and were on the market in ruby in the latter year.

136. A United States Glass Company item (reportedly #330 console bowl), $8\frac{1}{2}$" wide, $4\frac{1}{4}$" tall, lightly etched in this company's Kimberly decoration, satin-finished areas forming a design.

This decoration was advertised, reportedly about 1926, as available on ruby glass.

137. Apple with green stem, 5" tall, bought in 1976 at the Rainbow Art Glass Company factory, Huntington, West Virginia. Rainbow was evidently a subsidiary of Viking Glass Company at that time.

138. Cambridge Glass Company's Pristine #569 $9\frac{1}{2}$" crimped vase or bowl, made 1949-about 1956, in Carmen in 1950.

139. #2510 Sunray plate, evidently the "16 in. Flat Plate" Fostoria offered in ruby in 1935.

140. #$2470\frac{1}{2}$ $5\frac{1}{2}$" candlestick, 1935-1936, offered in ruby in 1935.

141. #2440 Lafayette 13" torte plate, 1935-1936, offered in ruby in 1935.

142. Heirloom #2729/540 10" oval bowl, made in ruby in 1961 and 1962. Reportedly this item was made in 1960 also, but not in ruby.

143. Heirloom #2726/311 candleholder, 3", made in ruby from 1961 to 1970.

144. #2517 6" handled lemon. This was available in ruby and other colors in 1935. Evidently it was available to at least 1939, as it appears on one reprinted catalogue page with Fostoria's #2564 Horse book end, which reportedly was introduced in 1939. 1935 is, however, the only year when this lemon is known to have been offered in ruby. All of the foregoing date and color information about the lemon dish apply also to the #2517 $5\frac{1}{4}$" handled sweetmeat and $5\frac{1}{4}$" handled bon bon not shown here, which are deeper dishes apparently made from the same mold as the handled lemon, then worked into square (the sweetmeat) and triangular (the bon bon) shapes.

Many years later, Fostoria made another item from the same mold, the #2517/135 handled bon bon. This was offered in ruby, teal green, and lavender in 1965 and 1967; by 1971 the color range had changed to crystal and ruby. From the poor line drawings of this item in Fostoria's catalogues of these years, and, from the dimensions given there (height 2½", length 5"), it seems to be round like the handled lemon in Figure 144, but a little deeper.

145. #2497/787 Flying Fish, made in ruby 1965-1967.

146 and 147. #2518 3 ounce footed cocktail, crystal foot with ruby bowl, and #2518 cocktail shaker, "Gold Top," 38 ounce. These two items were offered in ruby in a 1935 price list. They were offered also, without mention of ruby, on a later catalogue page, which includes #2496 Baroque, #2535, and #2536 items, all reportedly introduced in 1936. On another page the cocktail shaker is merely said to have a "Metal Top," so it may be that not all of the tops supplied by Fostoria were gold-colored.

148. CO 15/682 Colony sugar and cream. These were made in clear glass from 1940 or earlier to 1971, as the #2412 Colony footed sugar and footed cream (respectively 2412/679 and 2412/681, in the latter part of that period), were part of a popular set of tableware. Ruby Colony, however, seems to have been offered only later. There is no sign of it in Fostoria's 1975-1976 catalogue. In the 1982 catalogue and price list, three Colony items—this cream and sugar and a 6" footed bud vase CO 15/762—were offered in ruby; they were not designated in the price list as newly introduced, as various other items were. The sugar and cream were available in clear then also. The pieces in Figure 148 were bought new in 1982.

149. Heirloom #1515/279 16" oval centerpiece. This shape in Heirloom was reportedly made from 1959 to 1970. It was made in ruby 1961-1970.

150. Heirloom #2728/807 9" pitcher vase, made in ruby 1961-1970. Reportedly this shape was made in 1960 also, though not in ruby.

Figures 151-237: **Anchor Hocking Glass Corporation,** Lancaster, Ohio and elsewhere

This company was formed on December 31, 1937, by the merger of Hocking Glass Company of Lancaster, Ohio, with Anchor Cap Corporation of Long Island City, New York, and several other firms already controlled by these two. The resulting Anchor Hocking included glass factories from New Jersey to Indiana, and others have been added since then. The pre-merger Hocking Glass Company is credited with much machine-made tableware which has attracted collectors' interest; however, neither it nor any of the other glass factories involved—the majority of which were bottle and jar producers—appears to have made any red glass before being absorbed into Anchor Hocking.

Soon after its organization, Anchor Hocking Glass Corporation attained the capability to make red glass in large quantities by automatic machines. Anchor Hocking's glass, unlike most handmade ruby, used a formula in which the principal colorant was copper. The result, an evenly colored, dark red glass, was named Royal Ruby. The amount of Royal Ruby in existence today is tremendous, far more than the amount of red glass from any other manufacturer.

Royal Ruby was introduced in 1939. Made at a fraction of the cost of handmade red glass, it enabled Anchor Hocking to dominate the market for many years. Interesting information concerning its early years can be gleaned from wholesale catalogues issued by Butler Brothers, large "National Distributors of Dry Goods and General Merchandise." In their Winter and Holiday 1939 catalogue, about 22 different ruby items were offered, of which most were made by Imperial Glass Corporation, and a few by New Martinsville Glass Manufacturing Company. By the Summer 1940 edition, these handmade items had entirely disappeared; of about 14 red items shown, all appear to have been Anchor Hocking's. Further Butler Brothers catalogues continuing into 1942 show ruby from Anchor Hocking only.

Reportedly, difficulty in obtaining copper due to World War II, stopped production of Royal Ruby in 1943. Just when it was resumed is unclear, but tableware, vases and bottles were evidently being made in this color by 1950. According to Weatherman, odd pieces were offered as late as 1967.

In May, 1969, the word Glass was dropped from the firm's name, leaving it Anchor Hocking Corporation.

In 1977 Royal Ruby was again being made in about nine of the pieces made in this color earlier and items not previously made in this color. By that date there were many collectors interested in Royal Ruby. Apparently for that reason, Anchor Hocking advised collectors that all of the red pieces were being marked with the company's anchor trademark, that is, an anchor through an H. This mark is not found on earlier Royal Ruby items, except bottles. On the red items brought out in 1977, the mark is embossed quite small, and must sometimes have been overlooked by collectors; however, one report indicated that some items-notably 8³/₁₆" and 6¹/₁₆" plates, the punch cup, and the deep 4" bowl-were to be found unmarked in stores.

151. Tray, 14". Attributed to Anchor Hocking by Weatherman, this appears in 1941 and 1942 Butler Brothers catalogues in sets combining ruby with clear glass in an Anchor Hocking pattern.

152. Lazy susan, clear glass tray with five ruby inserts and a clear dish in the center. This is part of an Anchor Hocking set of tableware which, according to Weatherman, was made from approximately 1939 to 1941 and named Manhattan. The small dish in the center of Figure 152 appeared in wholesale catalogues in those three years. The inserts shown around it here were offered in 1941. Both were in clear glass; they were not grouped in the way shown in Figure 152.

153. 6¹/₂" nappy, apparently Anchor Hocking's Royal Ruby, no documentation available.

154. Sugar and creamer in the earliest of the three styles in which these items were made in Royal Ruby. This style was made from apparently as early as 1933 in clear glass to at least 1942; in red, these were on the market at least from 1940 to early 1942.

155. 4¹/₄" nappy and matching 8¹/₂" bowl, apparently Anchor Hocking's Royal Ruby; no more specific information is available.

156 and 157. 9" dinner plate and cup and saucer, made in Royal Ruby from 1940 to about 1950.

158. 9 ounce table tumbler, decorated in white with three musicians, captioned "Hoe Down". This appears to be Anchor Hocking's #3539 12 ounce tall tumbler shape, which was made in clear glass reportedly 1958-1961. There is a pitcher intended to

match, which is clear glass with this decoration in red; it is a shape made by Anchor Hocking in 1952 and reportedly the two preceding years. There is also a Royal Ruby tumbler, of shape matching the one here, with white decoration of dancers captioned "Do Si Do"; perhaps it and other related scenes were included in the same set.

159. Sherbet, apparently one of Anchor Hocking's. Notice the difference in the stem between this and Figure 162.

160. #3313 7 ounce footed sherbet. This was evidently on the market in Royal Ruby in 1950 and, at least in clear glass, from then to 1961.

161. Sugar and creamer, probably made by Anchor Hocking after the style shown in Figure 154.

162. Sherbet. This plain-stemmed style seems to be the one offered in wholesale catalogues from 1940 to 1942.

163. 32 ounce beer bottle, apparently Anchor Hockings, made in 1950; Royal Ruby is written on the bottom.

164. 16 ounce beer bottle, apparently Anchor Hocking's, made in 1963; Royal Ruby is written on the bottom.

165 and 165A. Fan snack set, crystal plate and ruby cup. Made by Anchor Hocking in Royal Ruby in the 1940s.

166 and 166A. Anchor Hocking's Royal Ruby punch bowl set. Bowl and stand, cup the same as figure 165, made in the 1940s.

167. 9" Hoover vase by Anchor Hocking.

168. Cigarette box by Anchor Hocking. Ruby lid with rose pattern and crystal box.

169. 3¹/₂", 4, 6, 8¹/₂" and 9 ounce Royal Ruby tumblers by Anchor Hocking. Some of these are Boopie pattern. Some having crystal bubble stems, made in the 1940s.

170 and 170A. 6¹/₂" ounce nappy, and 4¹/₂" ounce

berry in Royal Ruby. Made by Anchor Hocking in the 1940s.

171. Large bulbous vase by Anchor Hocking in Royal Ruby, made in the 1940s.

172. 4" ivy bowl in Royal Ruby by Anchor Hocking. Made in the 1940s.

173. 7" tidbit tray in Royal Ruby by Anchor Hocking.

174. 8" bowl, two handled in Royal Ruby. Coronation, Banded Ribbed, and Saxon are all names for the same pattern. Made by Anchor Hocking in the 1940s.

175. 10½" candy dish. Made in the 1940s by Anchor Hocking in Royal Ruby with chrome handle and three toes.

176. Crystal relish tray with five ruby inserts, crystal center dish and lid. Made by Anchor Hocking from 1936-1940 in the Old Cafe pattern.

177. 8½" Burple footd. bowl which has a 4⅝" matching desert dish (not shown). Made by Anchor Hocking in the 1940s.

178. Anchor Hockings Old Cafe cup and saucer. Ruby cup with crystal saucer made in the 1940s.

179. 6" Old Cafe sherbet plate. Made by Anchor Hocking in the 1940s in crystal only.

180. 6" Royal Ruby pickle dish. Made by Anchor Hocking in the 1940s.

181. 7" Royal Ruby pickle dish. Made by Anchor Hocking in the 1940s.

182. 9" Old Cafe Bon-Bon. Made also in crystal by Anchor Hocking in the 1940s.

183. 9" Royal Ruby celery tray. Made by Anchor Hocking in the 1940s.

184. 5½" Old Cafe cereal bowl. Made by Anchor Hocking in the 1940s.

185. Anchor Hocking's Old Cafe dessert bowl made in the 1940s.

186. 5½" Old Cafe berry bowl. Made by Anchor Hocking in the 1940s.

187. Anchor Hocking's Old Cafe covered candy dish. Ruby lid with crystal dish, made in the 1940s.

188. Mustard jar, by Anchor Hocking. Has ruby lid, with opening for spoon, and crystal base. Made in the 1940s.

189. 8" Old Cafe covered candy dish. Ruby lid with crystal base. Made by Anchor Hocking in the 1940s.

190. 9 oz. Georgian tumbler. Made by Anchor Hocking in the 1940s.

191. 80 oz. Georgian Pitcher. Made by Anchor Hocking in the 1970s.

192. 9 oz. High Point tumbler. Made by Anchor Hocking in the 1940s.

193. 80 oz. High Point pitcher. Made by Anchor Hocking in the 1940s.

194. 8 oz. Royal tumbler. Made by Anchor Hocking in the 1940s.

195. 80 oz. Royal pitcher. Made by Anchor Hocking in the 1940s.

196. 4½" high Hobnail tumbler by Anchor Hocking. Made in the 1930s in very poor color.

197. 8½" high Hobnail pitcher by Anchor Hocking. Made in the 1930s in very poor color.

198. 8 oz. Royal Ruby tumbler. Made by Anchor Hocking in the 1940s.

199. 80 oz. Royal Ruby pitcher. Made by Anchor Hocking in the 1940s.

200. 16 oz. Provincial (also known as Bubble) iced tea glass. Made by Anchor Hocking in 1963.

201. 64 oz. Provincial (also known as Bubble) pitcher. Made by Anchor Hocking in 1963.

202. 10 oz. Royal Ruby tumbler. Made by Anchor Hocking from 1938 to 1966, and again in 1977.

203. 96 oz. Royal Ruby upright pitcher. Made by Anchor Hocking from 1938 to 1966 and again in 1977.

204. 9 oz. Swirl tumbler. Made by Anchor Hocking from 1938 to 1966, and again in 1977.

205. Anchor Hocking's Swirl tilted pitcher. Made from 1938 to 1966, and again in 1977.

206. 5 oz. Royal Ruby juice glass. Made by Anchor Hocking from 1938 to 1966, and again in 1977.

207. 22 oz. Royal Ruby tilted juice pitcher. Made by Anchor Hocking from 1938 to 1966, and again in 1977.

208. 10½" Oyster & Pearl fruit bowl. Made by Anchor Hocking from 1938 to 1940.

209. 6½" Royal Ruby vase. Made by Anchor Hocking in the 1940s.

210. 6⅜" Harding vase. Made by Anchor Hocking in the 1940s.

211. 13½" Oyster & Pearl plate. Made by Anchor Hocking from 1938 to 1940.

212. 8" berry bowl. Made by Anchor Hocking in the 1940s.

213. 5" small bowl. Made by Anchor Hocking in the 1940s.

214. 6½" Oyster & Pearl bowl. Made by Anchor Hocking from 1938 to 1940.

215. 5¼" Oyster & Pearl nappy with one handle. Made by Anchor Hocking from 1938 to 1940.

216. 3½" Oyster & Pearl candlestick. Made by Anchor Hocking from 1938 to 1940.

217. 6½" Royal Ruby leaf dish. Made by Anchor Hocking in the 1940s.

218. 5½" Sandwich bowl. Made by Anchor Hocking from 1939 to 1940.

219. 8" Sandwich scalloped bowl. Made by Anchor Hocking from 1939 to 1940.

220. 5" Royal Ruby leaf dish. Made by Anchor Hocking in the 1940s.

221. 4" fluted vase by Anchor Hocking, made in the 1940s.

222. Anchor Hocking's Bubble cup and saucer. Also known as Bullseye Provincial pattern, made in 1960.

223. 9⅜" Bubble plate. Made by Anchor Hocking in 1960. Also known as Bullseye, and Provincial pattern.

224. 4" Bubble fruit bowl. Made by Anchor Hocking in 1960. Also known as Bullseye or Provincial pattern.

225. 8⅜" Bubble berry bowl. Made by Anchor Hocking in 1960. Also known as Bullseye or Provincial pattern.

226. 4½" Royal Ruby scalloped berry bowl. Made by Anchor Hocking in the 1940s.

227. 8" Royal Ruby scalloped berry bowl. Made by Anchor Hocking in the 1940s.

228. Square saucer. Made by Anchor Hocking in the 1940s.

229. Square cup. Made by Anchor Hocking in the 1940s.

230. 7¾" Square plate. Made by Anchor Hocking in the 1940s.

231. 4½" Square berry bowl. Made by Anchor Hocking in the 1940s.

232. 8½" Square berry bowl. Made by Anchor Hocking in the 1940s.

233. 9" Round plate. Made by Anchor Hocking in the 1940s.

234. Round cup and saucer. Made by Anchor Hocking in the 1940s.

235. 7³/₄" Round luncheon plate. Made by Anchor Hocking in the 1940s.

236. Round cream and sugar. Made by Anchor Hocking in the 1940s.

237. 8" vegetable bowl. Made by Anchor Hocking in the 1940s.

Figures 238-639: **Various Companies**

238. 10¹/₂" Munsell bowl with silver deposit. Made by Imperial in 1950.

239. 3 light candelabrum. Made by Imperial in 1931.

240. 9 oz. Hobnail table tumbler. Made by Imperial in 1931.

241. 8¹/₂" Pillar Flute oval celery bowl, shown in metal holder. Made by Imperial in 1931.

242. 10 oz. #22 Astaire goblet. Made by Duncan amd Miller Glass Company in 1931.

243. 7¹/₂" Molly bon-bon tray. By Imperial in 1931.

244. 5" Sugar Cane line basket bowl. Made by Imperial in 1931.

245. 4¹/₂" Tradition finger bowl. Made by Imperial in 1931.

246. Imperial's #600 toothpick holder, made about 1966.

247. Imperial's cream and sugar, made in 1931.

248. 6" box and cover, marked IG on bottom. Made by Imperial from 1972 to 1975.

249. Imperial's lamp, paper label on bottom, grape pattern.

250. 4¹/₂" salt and pepper, grape pattern. Made by Imperial in 1950.

251. Imperial's bud vase, grape pattern.

252. Imperial's fluted bowl, grape pattern.

253. 6¹/₂" Cape Cod fruit bowl, by Imperial.

254. 7" Cape Cod salad plate, by Imperial.

255. Imperial's Cape Cod saucer.

256. Imperial's Cape Cod goblet.

257. Imperial's Cape Cod wine goblet.

258. 8" Mount Vernon plate by Imperial.

259. 7" Pillar Flute shallow compote with metal stand. Made by Imperial in 1931.

260. 6" Pillar Flute vase. Made by Imperial in 1931.

261. Pillar Flute cream and sugar. Made by Imperial in 1931.

262. 7" Pillar Flute crimped bon-bon. Made by Imperial in 1931.

263. 5" Pillar Flute crimped bowl. Made by Imperial in 1931.

264. 4¹/₂" Pillar Flute 2 handled jelly. Made by Imperial in 1931.

265. 6¹/₂" Pillar Flute 2 handled pickle. Made by Imperial in 1931.

266. Imperial's Pillar Flute mayonnaise, made in 1931.

267. 5" Pillar Flute bowl. Made by Imperial in 1931.

268. 12 oz. Reeded #701 tumbler, by Imperial.

269. 80 oz. Reeded #701 pitcher. Made by Imperial in 1935.

270. 6" Reeded #701 rose bowl. Made by Imperial in 1939.

271. Imperial's Hazen cream and sugar, made in 1939 in ruby.

272. 8" Molly plate. Made in ruby by Imperial in 1936.

273. Imperial's Fish canape plate, with unidentified tumbler, made in the 1930s.

274. 6½" Sugar Cane nappy. Made by Imperial in 1931.

275. 7½" Sugar Cane plate. Made by Imperial in 1931.

276. 9¼" Laced Edge bowl. Made in ruby by Imperial in 1936.

277. 7¾" Laced Edge bowl, by Imperial.

278. 4¼" Genie vase, by Imperial.

279. Imperial's Apple marmalade set with metal lid, blown jar, and pressed plate.

280. 7¾" Laced Edge nappy, by Imperial.

281. Imperial's Newbound twin candlestick.

282. 16" Sandwich plate. Made by the Indiana Glass Company from the 1960s through the 1970s.

283. 13" Sandwich footed cakeplate, also in blue and green. Made by Indiana from the 1960s through the 1970s.

284. 9 oz. goblet, by Indiana.

285. Sandwich "lite on stem" in very deep ruby. Made for Tiara by Indiana in the 1970s.

286. Indiana's Sandwich sugar and creamer.

287. Indiana's Sandwich cup and saucer.

288. 8¾" Sandwich plate by Indiana.

289. 8¼" 3 footed bowl.

290. Cambridge's salt and pepper shakers with Farberware holders.

291. 11½" Candlewick pastry tray. Called Regal Red Rare by Virginia Scott, in January 1985's, *Glass Review*. Made by Imperial from 1962 to 1963.

292. 12" American Sweetheart salver. Made by Macbeth-Evans from 1930 through 1936.

293. 4½" footed sherbet with no pattern. Made by Macbeth-Evans from 1930 through 1936.

294. 15½" American Sweetheart Server, rare. Made by Macbeth-Evans from 1930 through 1936.

295. 8½" Rock Crystal candlestick with an octagon base. Made by McKee from 1920 to the 1930s.

296. 12 oz. Rock Crystal No.2 concave iced tea. Made by McKee from 1920 through the 1930s.

297. 3½" oz. Rock Crystal low footed parfait. Made by McKee from 1920 through the 1930s.

298. 5" Rock Crystal finger bowl. Made by McKee from 1920 through the 1930s.

299. Macbeth-Evans' American saucer, made from 1930 through 1936, is hard to find.

300. Macbeth-Evans' Sweetheart cup. This rare cup was made from 1930 through 1936.

301. 8" Sweetheart plate. This rare plate was made by Macbeth-Evans from 1930 through 1936.

302. 13" Rock Crystal sandwich server. This sandwich server is rare and has a center handle. It was made by McKee from 1920 through the 1930s.

303. 10 oz. Rock Crystal footed sugar. Made by McKee from 1920 through the 1930s.

304. 9 oz. Rock Crystal footed creamer was made by McKee from 1920 through the 1930s.

305. McKee's Rock Crystal saucer was made from 1920 through the 1930s.

306. 9½" Moondrops cocktail shaker with metal top. Made by New Martinsville from 1932 through 1940.

307. 8½" Moondrops decanter. Made by New Martinsville from 1932 through 1940.

308. 9½" Moondrops 3 footed bowl. Made by New Martinsville from 1932 through 1940.

309. 4 oz. Moondrops wine goblet. Made in New Martinsville from 1932 through 1940.

310. 5¼" Moondrop "triple-lite." This was made by New Martinsville from 1932 through 1940 and is hard to find.

311. 5¼" Moondrops wings candle holder. This was made by New Martinsville from 1932 through 1940 and is hard to find.

312. 12" Moondrops footed bowl. Made by New Martinsville from 1932 through 1940.

313. 8½" Moondrops 3 footed relish dish. Made by New Martinsville from 1932 through 1940.

314. 2⅝" Moondrops footed sherbet. Made by New Martinsville from 1932 through 1940.

315. 9¾" Moondrops Oval Vegetable. Made by New Martinsville from 1932 through 1940.

316. 2¾" sugar and 3¾" creamer in Moondrops. Made by New Martinsville from 1932 to 1940.

317. 4 oz. Moondrops wine tumbler. Made by New Martinsville from 1932 through 1940.

318. 4¾" high Moondrops rocket wine tumbler. Made by New Martinsville from 1932 to 1940.

319. 9 oz. Moondrops water tumbler. Made by New Martinsville from 1932 through 1940.

320. 6" Moondrops butter dish, also comes with winged lid. Made by New Martinsville from 1932 through 1940.

321. 4½" Moondrops 3 footed candy dish with metal lid. Made by New Martinsville from 1932 through 1940.

322. 8½" candlestick, with metal stem. Company unknown, probably made between 1932 to around 1940.

323. 6" Radiance stemmed bon-bon, with chrome stem and crimped bowl. Made by New Martinsville in 1937 or later.

324. #412 Bee's Knees or Crows Foot Square sandwich tray with silver deposit. Made by Paden City Glass Mfg. Co. in the 1930s.

325. 14" Radiance Torte plate, used as liner for fruit bowl. Made by New Martinsville in 1937 or later.

326. 6" Radiance crimped bon-bon. Made by New Martinsville in 1937 or later.

327. 9 oz. Radiance tumbler. Made by New Martinsville in 1937 or later.

328. 4 oz. Radiance punch cup. Made by New Martinsville in 1937 or later.

329. 1 oz. Radiance cordial by New Martinsville.

330. 7" Radiance pickle dish. Made by New Martinsville in 1937 or later.

331. 2¾" sugar, 2¾" creamer, 7½" tray, in Moondrops pattern. Made by New Martinsville from 1932 through 1940.

332. Ashtray.

333. Moondrops cup shown on sherbet plate. Made by New Martinsville from 1932 through 1940.

334. 443-1 SJ Swan. Made by New Martinsville probably in the 1940s.

335. 160 oz. Radiance punch bowl. Made by New Martinsville in 1937 or later.

336. 14" Radiance liner. Made by New Martinsville in 1937 or later.

337. 12" Radiance punch ladle (rare). Made by new Martinsville in 1937 or later.

338. 4 oz. Radiance punch cup. Made by New Martinsville in 1937 or later.

339. 12" crimped bowl on stand. Made by New Martinsville in 1937 or later.

340. 7½" by 5½" tall, Radiance candleholder. Made by New Martinsville in 1937 or later.

341. Radiance 5 piece service: cream and sugar set, tray, and salt and pepper. Made in New Martinsville in 1937 or later.

342. New Martinsville's Radiance cup and saucer, made in 1937 or later.

343. 7" Radiance plate. Made by New Martinsville in 1937 or later.

344. 8" Radiance 3 compartment relish dish. Made by New Martinsville in 1937 or later.

345. 7" Radiance 2 compartment relish dish. Made by New Martinsville in 1937 or later.

346. 11" Janice fruit bowl. Made by New Martinsville or Viking Glass Company between 1936 and 1984.

347. 5½" Janice candlestick by New Martinsville.

348. 12" Janice 2 handled plate. Made by New Martinsville in 1984.

349. 5½" Swan Janice, swan candy box, cover missing. Made by New Martinsville, possibly in the 1940s.

350. 8" Janice plate. Made in New Martinsville in 1936 or later.

351. Janice cup and saucer. Made in New Martinsville in 1936 or later.

352. 12" Swan Janice 4521-1 SJ, swan. Made by New Martinsville in 1936 or later.

353. 8" set: red handled basket with #412-1 SJ swan. Made in New Martinsville possibly in the 1940s.

354. 7 oz. Janice goblet. Made by New Martinsville in 1936 or later.

355. 2¾" Janice creamer. Made by New Martinsville in 1936 or later.

356. 3¾" Janice low sherbet. Made by New Martinsville in 1936 or later.

357. 7" Janice 2 handled plate. Made by Viking Glass Company in 1984 and 1985.

358. 7½" Janice footed candy dish. Made by Viking Glass Company in 1984 and 1985.

359. 6" Janice 2 compartment relish. Made by New Martinsville in 1984 and 1985.

360. Paden City's Largo 2 handled plate, made from 1937 through 1951.

361. #888 Plume 3 piece epergne. Made by Paden City probably in the 1039s.

362. 6¾" high, 9¾" wide Largo Line #220 compote. Made by Paden City in the 1930s.

363. 14 oz. Big Shot tumbler. Came in 3 sizes with matching decanter. Made by Imperial Glass Corporation in the 1950s.

364. Probably #890 Crows Foot candleholder. Made by Paden City probably in the 1930s.

365. 5¼" by 3¼" Hostmaster ice tub, Made by New Martinsville in 1935.

366. 11½" Hostmaster line cocktail shaker. Made by New Martinsville in 1935.

367. Largo #220 compote. By Paden City in 1937.

368. #215 Glades set includes 5¼" perfume, 4" powder box and crystal tray of a vanity set also called Sun Set. Made by Paden City in 1936.

369. New Martinsville's Hostmaster line, sugar and creamer, made in 1935.

370. 7" #215½ Glades cordial decanter with silver

deposit and poppy design. Made by Paden City from 1936 through 1954.

371. Nerva 2 handled plate, has a feather pattern on the bottom. Made by Paden City in the 1930s.

372. 10½" Crows Foot vase. Made by Paden City probably in the 1930s.

373. 10½", Lindburgh #7192D footed cake salver. Made by Imperial, probably in the 1930s.

374. 5¾" candlesticks with unknown pattern, made about 1935.

375. 6" Old English bowl. Made by Imperial from about 1936 through 1939.

376. Imperial's Old English mayonnaise, made in 1939 in ruby.

377. Imperial's Old English candlestick, made in 1939 in ruby.

378. Imperial's Old English candy jar (cover missing), made in 1939 in ruby.

379. Paden City's Popeye and Olive #994 goblet, made in 1932.

380. Paden City's Popeye and Olive #994 high foot sherbet, made in 1932.

381. 5½" #888 Plume candleholder, matches epergne, Figure 361. Made by Paden City in 1930.

382. Paden City's #991 Penny Line cordial, made in 1932.

383. Possibly #451 Shaeffer cup. Probably made by Imperial Glass in the 1930s.

384. 5½" plate. Company and date unkown.

385. Paden City's Penny Line #991 cup, made in 1932.

386. Paden City's Penny Line #991 sugar and creamer, made in 1932.

387. 4 oz. Penny line #991 wine goblet. Made by Paden City in 1932.

388. 12¼" #37 Moondrops oval platter. Made by New Martinsville in 1932.

389. 10" Wotta Line low foot comport with Irwin Etching. Made by Paden City in 1933.

390. 8" Wotta Line plate with Irwin etching. Made by Paden City in 1932.

391. 6" #991 Penny line ccreal bowl. Made by Paden City in 1932.

392. 8" #836 Futura Line plate. Made by the Canton Glass Company, Marion, Indiana, from the 1930s through 1954.

393. 10½" #991 Penny line handled sandwich tray. Made by Paden City in 1932.

394. 6½" Gadroon #3500/54 low comport. Made by Cambridge from 1933 through 1949.

395. 4½" Wotta line mayonnaise bowl. Made by Paden City in 1933.

396. 8" plate. Company and date unknown.

397. 11½" #37 Moondrops celery dish. Made in New Martinsville in 1932 or later.

398. 18" City Lights plate. Possibly made by Paden City or Canton Glass Company from 1940 to 1954.

399. Paden City's #184 vase, made in the 1930s.

400. New Martinsville's #18 Crystal Eagle sugar and creamer, made in 1936.

401. 13¼" #18 Crystal Eagle oval bowl. Made by New Martinsville in 1936.

402. 7" #18 Crystal Eagle candleholder. Made by New Martinsville in 1936.

403. Cornucopia, Company and date unknown.

404. 2 oz. Radiance cordial. Made by New Martinsville in the 1930s.

405. New Martinsville's Radiance decanter, made in 1937 or later.

406. #7643 cordial, made by Morgantown Glass Works, Morgantown, West Virginia.

407. Newport cup and saucer. Maker is unknown; sold by Pitman-Dreitzer and Company in 1935.

408. 5¹/₂" Janice candleholder. Made by New Martinsville in 1936 or later.

409. 10" #412 Crow's Foot Square or Bees Knees stemmed comport. Made by Paden City in the 1930s.

410. 10" #412 Crow's Foot Square bowl. Made by Paden City in the 1930s.

411. 9¹/₂" #890 Crow's Foot (Round) platter. Made by Paden City in the 1930s.

412. 11¹/₂" #412 Crow's Foot Square console bowl. Made by Paden City in the 1930s.

413. Paden City's #412 Crow's Foot Square sugar and creamer, made in the 1930s.

414. 7" #412 Crow's Foot Square tall comport with Orchid etched pattern. Made by Paden City in the 1930s.

415. 8¹/₄" #890 Crow's Foot Round plate. Made by Paden city in the 1930s.

416. 7" Crow's Foot Round salad plate. Made by Paden City in the 1930s.

417. 9" #890 Crow's Foot Round oblong bowl. Made by Paden City in the 1930s.

418. 12¹/₄" #890 Crow's Footed Round low foot cake salver. Made by Paden City in the 1930s.

419. 10" #412 Crow's Foot Square handled sandwich tray. Made by Paden City in the 1930s.

420. 10³/₄" #890 Crow's Foot Round handled sandwich tray. Made by Paden City in the 1930s.

421. 9" #895 Lucy handled bowl. Probably made by Paden City in 1935.

422. 5¹/₄" #412 Crow's Foot Square candlestick. Made by Paden City in the 1930s.

423. 4¹/₂" #890 Crow's Foot Round cream soup. Made by Paden City in the 1930s.

424. 9¹/₂" #890 Crow's Foot Round bowl. Made by Paden City in the 1930s.

425. 7" #412¹/₂ candy box and lid. Made by Paden City about 1932 through 1954.

426. Paden City's #890 Crow's Foot Round cup and #412 Crow's Foot Square saucer, made in the 1930s.

427. 8¹/₂" #412 Crow's Foot Square plate. Made by Paden City in the 1930s.

428. 5¹/₄" #412 Crow's Foot Square dessert. Made by Paden City in the 1930s.

429. 7" Biscuit Jar with satin finish, silver band, lid and bear handle. Probably made by Consolidated Lamp and Glass Company, Coraopolis, PA, possibly in the early 1900s.

430. Bead and Drape satin sugar bowl with silver lid and handles. Made by Pittsburgh Lamp, Brass and Glass Company about 1902.

431. Satin oil lamp with lions heads in glass.

432. Satin oil lamp made by Pittsburgh Lamp, Brass and Glass Company about 1902.

433. Satin oil lamp, square.

434. Victorian 12³/₄" Lustre, made from 1875 through 1910.

435. Victorian silver candy dish with ruby liner.

436. Victorian Honey Bee. Came from New York's STORK CLUB and is silver with a ruby body.

437. Victorian sugar and creamer. Silver with ruby liners.

438. Victorians barber bottle with ruby overlay.

439. Victorian barber dispenser with ruby overlay.

440. 4" sugar shaker in a Hobnail pattern.

441. Victorian basket with silver mesh and ruby liner.

442. Victorian egg box. Ruby overlay with painted flowers, hinged.

443. Victorian silver mustard with ruby liner.

444. Victorian potty souvenir, ruby flashed.

445. Victorian perfume. Divided perfume and smelling salts, metal hinged lid.

446. Victorian cup plate with ruby overlay. Has a picture of a gazebo.

447. Chrome decanter, comes in a set with 6 wine goblets. See 447A.

447A. Wine goblet on chrome stem.

448. Chrome decanter, comes in a set with 6 wine goblets. See 448A.

448A. Wine goblet on chrome stem.

449. Chrome decanter, comes with 6 wine goblets. See 449A.

449A. Wine goblet on chrome stem.

450. New Martinsville's Moondrops chrome decanter, made in 1932. Comes with 6 wine goblets. See 450A.

450A. New Martinsville's Moondrops wine goblet, made in 1932. Comes in a set of 6.

451. Ice bucket. Silver overlay with grapes, chrome handle and tongs.

452. Footed wine goblet. Silver overlay with grapes; that matches the ice bucket #451.

453. Wine decanter which comes with 6 goblets and tray. See 453A.

453A. Wine goblet.

454. Decanter made in the 1930s.

455. 12³⁄₄" Rooster decanter and 3¹⁄₂" stopper made by Morgantown in 1929. Comes with matching wine goblets. See 455A.

455A. 4" high glasses to accompany Rooster decanter. Crystal rooster stems with ruby cups. Made by Morgantown in 1929.

456. 32 oz. decanter with gold or silver rings and a metal lid. Made in the 1930s. Has 6 matching wine goblets. See 456A.

456A. Wine goblet with gold or silver rings. Comes in sets of 6.

457. 32 oz. decanter by New Martinsville, made in the 1930s.

458. 32 oz. Pewter decanter. Has matching goblets, see 458A.

458A. 9 oz. pewter goblet.

459. 9¹⁄₂" pie shell for baking, by Pyrex.

460. 11¹⁄₂" dripolator coffee pot, metal stand, handle and lid. Cord wrapped in re thread and marked H & H, made USA.

461. 16 oz. measuring cup.

462. 32 oz. Roly Poly hostess pitcher. Made by MacBeth-Evans in 1932.

463. 8¹⁄₂" Bread baking pan by Pyrex. Marked DD-26 (Trademark).

464. Vinegar cruet.

465. 32 oz. Bell Shaped fruit jar. Has writting on the bottom "Do not use for canning." Made in 1973.

466. Tiara's Sunset Leaf console set with 5" candlesticks. Made by Indiana Glass Company in 1978.

467. Tiara's Jar and Cover. Made by Indiana Glass in 1974.

468, 468A and 468B. Wheaton jars. "Wheaton" on the bottom. May be used as spice jars or shakers. Some have cork stoppers or plastic inserts.

469. Wheaton's decanter with "Wheaton" on the bottom.

470. 9¼" divided dish with four sections.

471. 10" Sheffield salver with metal handle. Made by Fenton in the 1930s.

472. 10¾" dinner plate with 3 sections. Made by Paden City in the 1930s.

473. 6¼" Sheffield ice bucket with metal handle and tongs. Made by Fenton in the 1930s.

474. 7¼" Sheffield bowl. Made by Fenton in the 1930s.

475. 9½" Sheffield ruffled bowl. Made by Fenton in the 1930s.

476. 3-section relish dish with crystal handle.

477. Maker unknown.

478. 3 section relish dish.

479. 4x7, oblong 5- section divided dish.

480. 14" liner.

481. Plate.

482. Sugar and creamer, matches plate 478.

483. Cup and saucer, same as 481.

484. 8" plate, same as 481.

485. 8 oz. mug.

486. 10" Rachel vase. Made by Anchor Hocking in the 1940s.

487. 11" Rachel punchbowl. Made by Anchor Hocking in the 1940s. Has a liner, see 487A.

487A. 14" Rachel liner. Made by Anchor Hocking in the 1940s.

488. 12¼" Rachel oval bowl. Made by Anchor Hocking in the 1940s.

489. Plate.

490. Corniucopia with a crystal base.

491. Corniucopia. Famous Pierpoint Ruby, by Gunderson Glass Works, New Bedford, Mass.

492. Bowl, made by Paden City in the 1930s.

493. 4½" stand. Made by Cambridge from 1948 through 1953.

494. 6½" satin wall vase, very rare. Made by Tiffin in 1926.

495. Imperial's bowl.

496. Lion planter, flower pot and saucer.

497. L.E. Smith egg plate. Holds 6 eggs. These were for Home Party Sales, but were never used. Very few were made. Bought from LeVay Distributing Company in Southern Illinois.

498. Paden City's divided plate.

499. 5½" 2- handled planter basket.

500. 13¾" high electric lamp.

501. 16½" high oil lamp with a ruby stained base and ruby chimney.

502. 12" oil lamp with ruby stained base and chimney.

503. 9½" electric lamp. Made by Fenton in 1931.

504. 9" oil lamp bought at Viking Glass. Made in 1976.

505. Viking's satin oil lamp. Bought at company. Made in 1976.

506. 8¼" Rose Wreath oil lamp. Made by

Pittsburgh Lamp, Brass and Glass Company. Shown on book cover; converted to electric.

507. Oil lamp with milk glass base and ruby chimney.

508. 4" miniature oil lamp with clear chimney.

508A. 4¹/₂" miniature oil lamp with ruby flashed chimney.

509. 8¹/₄" Beehive kerosene lamp with ruby bottom, scarce. Made by Mantle Lamp Company from 1937 through 1938.

510. 15¹/₂" wide, 21" tall Victorian electric lamp, by Pittsburgh Lamp Company.

511, 511A, 511B and 511C. Victorian salt shakers.
(511) 2¹/₂" satin salt shaker.
(511A) 2¹/₂" plain salt shaker.
(511B) 3" plain salt shaker.
(511C) 2¹/₂" plain slat shaker.

512. 13" vase with heavy gold and applied flowers. Label on vase. Made in Czechoslovakia.

513. 4 oz. musical decanter from Japan. Original label reading Ardill. Plays *Cabaret* when you lift it. Made by Cenwide Glass Co. in the 1970s. Comes with 6 wine tumblers. See 513A.

513A. Wine tumbler from Japan. Made by Cenwide Glass Co. in the 1970s in a set of 6.

514. 18" tall Murano Glass decanter set, from Italy. Bought from distributor in 1982. Still has original label. Comes in a set of 7. See 514A for goblets.

514A. 6¹/₂" goblet, from Italy. Comes in a set of 6. Bought from distributor in 1982.

515. 9¹/₂" vase with gold overlay from Czechoslovakia.

516. 5 oz. wine goblet from Czechoslovakia. Matches 512.

517. 3" nut dish with enameled floral design.

518. 5" Bohemian glass bell with gold filigree design from Czechoslovakia. Original label. Made in 1980.

519. 6³/₄" footed compote with enameled cameo from Czechoslovakia.

520. 6³/₄" Victorian footed compote with gold overlay.

521. 3¹/₂" tall drum bank with silver casing, drumsticks and ruby celluloid insert. Made in the 1930s.

522. 6¹/₈" Budda that says Gillinder on bottom.

523. 10¹/₂" x 8¹/₂" Victorian double ink well. Plate has 2 holes for jars. Metal lids have enameled pattern.

524. 6¹/₄" Victorian souvenir shovel, ruby flashed.

525. 6" Victorian souvenir tomahawk. Flased, says Souvenir of Hagler, Nebraska. Owned by my parents, Mr. and Mrs. Z.H. Baxter. Made in 1915.

526. Venetian 9" high Dolphin stemmed compote with flecks of gold in glass.

527. Venetian 15¹/₂" tall 13¹/₄" wide Epergene, rare. Comes in four pieces.

528. Venetian 12" swan handled vase.

529. Venetian 9³/₄" dancers.

530. Venetian 4¹/₂" Dolphin candlesticks.

531. Venetian 8" Cornucopia with colored flowers applied.

532. Venetian 8¹/₂" Cornucopia.

533. Venetian 5" basket.

534. Venetian 5³/₄" Grapes candlestick. Came from Classic Galleries, Frank Walker Jr. and Associates, Wheeler, TX. Made from 1790 through 1820.

535. Venetian 4 oz. Dolphin wine goblet. Was a wedding present, still in original box. Disliked the Aunt who gave them, so they were never used. Made in 1940.

536. Venetian 8³/₄" swan stem goblet.

537. Venetian 7¹/₂" long swan.

538. Venetian 7³/₄" dolphin vase.

539. Venetian 6" lady bell. Black face, ruby bell. An extraordinary piece in Venetian glass.

540. 7" owl glimmer. Made by Viking Glass from 1981 through 1982.

541. 7" Glimmer pot bellied stove, sold at wholesale florists. Made by Viking Glass in 1971.

542. 9" Viking's Mama Duck.

543. 5" Viking's Mini Duck.

544. 9" Glimmer snowman. Made by Viking Glass in 1983.

545. 16" vase. Made by Viking glass in 1982.

546. 3³/₄" bell. Made by Viking Glass from 1984 through 1985.

547. Strawberry paperweight.

548. 3¹/₂" Yesteryear bell by Viking Glass.

549. 8¹/₂" pear by Viking Glass.

550. 3³/₄" apple by Viking Glass.

551. 3³/₄" bell in the shape of the Liberty Bell, by Viking Glass.

552. 6¹/₂" swan. Made by Viking Glass from 1984 through 1985.

553. 6¹/₂" Mt. Vernon compote. Made by Viking Glass from 1984 through 1985.

554. 5" bell. Made by Viking Glass from 1984 through 1985.

555. 4" bell. Made by Viking Glass from 1984 through 1985.

556. 7" bon-bon. Made by Viking Glass from 1984 through 1985.

557. Diamond and Thumbprint salt and pepper shakers. Made by Viking Glass from 1984 through 1985.

558. 7" bon bon. Made by Viking Glass from 1984 through 1985.

559. 6" Georgian bell. Made by Viking Glass from 1984 through 1985.

560. 4³/₄" Mt. Vernon bell. Made by Viking Glass from 1984 through 1985.

561. Viking's mushroom, original label.

562. Westmoreland's Fluted butter dish, made in the 1980s.

563. 5³/₄" Laced edge rosebowl. Made by Westmoreland from 1980 through 1983.

564. 4¹/₂" laced edge candlestick. Made by Westmoreland from 1980 through 1983.

565. 8¹/₂" Cherry cracker jar. Made by Westmoreland from 1980 through 1983.

566. 8¹/₂" Mary Gregory plate. Summer, winter, autumn, and fall patterns, hand painted. Made by Westmoreland from 1980 through 1983.

567. 7¹/₄" Mary Gregory laced heart with sunbonnet girl. Hand painted. Made by Westmoreland from 1980 through 1983.

568. 6¹/₂" Hobnail butter dish. Distributed by LeVay only. Made by Westmoreland in the 1980s.

569. 5" Mary Gregory basket with summer scene. Made by Westmoreland from 1980 through 1983.

570. 4¹/₄" treasure chest with summer scene. Made by Westmoreland from 1980 through 1983.

571. 6½" Floral bell. Made by Westmoreland in 1977.

572. 4½" square Mary Gregory jewel box with summer scene. Made by Westmoreland from 1980 through 1983.

573. 5" Mary Gregory bell with sunbonnet girl. Made by Westmoreland from 1980 through 1983.

574. Square candy box. Made by Westmoreland from 1980 through 1983.

575. 5" slipper, square-toed, painted shoelace. Made by Westmoreland from 1980 through 1983.

576. 8¾" Buzz Star vase. Made by Westmoreland in 1981.

577. 8½" Elite vase. Made by Westmoreland in 1981.

578. 14" Maple Leaf basket. Made by Westmoreland in 1982.

579. 10½" Maple Leaf bowl. Made by Westmoreland in 1982.

580. Westmoreland's 3-footed candy dish with shell handle, made in 1982.

581. 8½" English Hobnail cube butter. Distributed by LeVay only. Only 800 were made. Made by Westmoreland in the 1980's.

582. 8 oz. English Hobnail tumbler. Made by Westmoreland in 1981.

583. 16 oz. milk pitcher. Made by Westmoreland in 1982.

584. Vase, made in 1982 by Westmorcland.

585. 5¼" Quilted cruet. Made by Westmoreland in 1982.

586. 3" cup plates with butterfly and heart pattern. Made by Westmoreland in 1982.

587. 6" basket. Made by Westmoreland in the 1980s.

588. 5¼" Strutting Peacock sugar and cream, limited edition. Made by Westmoreland in the 1980s.

589. 12" Moon and Star banana boat. Made by L.G. Wright from 1974 through 1981.

590. 8 oz. Double Ring satin goblet, also has matching pitcher. Made by L.G. Wright from 1974 through 1981.

591. 13½" long, 6½" wide, 6" tall Daisy and Button sled. Made by L.G. Wright from 1974 to 1981.

592. 8¾" Eyewinker Marmalade. Made by L.G. Wright from 1974 through 1981.

593. 4¼" Sweetheart fairy lamp. Made by L.G. Wright from 1974 through 1981.

594 and 594A. 4 oz. Hobnail 5¼" sugar and 3" cream. Made by L.G. Wright from 1974 - 1981.

595. Daisy and Button bell candy dish. 5" bell-shaped lid, 5" dish. Made by L.G. Wright from 1974 through 1981.

596. 4 oz. Stipple Star wine goblet. Made by L.G. Wright from 1974 through 1981.

597. 3¼" Mirror and Rose salt and pepper. Made by L.G. Wright from 1974 through 1981.

598. 2½" Hobnail salt and pepper. Made by L.G. Wright from 1974 through 1981.

599. 4 oz. Panelled Grape punch cup. Made by L.G. Wright from 1974 through 1981.

600. Pitch pipe, celluloid.

601. 4 oz. Moon and Star syrup pitcher. Made by L.G. Wright in 1982.

602. 6" long Daisy and Button boat. Made by L.G. Wright from 1974 through 1981.

603. 3¾" Sweetheart fluted candy. Made by L.G. Wright in 1976.

604. 10" Capital plate. Carnival is stamped on the plate. Made by Imperial in 1969.

605. 7½" Madonna of RoseHedge Mother's Day plate. Limited Edition, #9 of Series. Made by Fenton in 1979.

606. 8¾" Christmas plates for the 12 days of Christmas. A different color was issued for each year—red was the 12th. Carnival is stamped on the plate. Made by Imperial in 1980.

607. 6½" Red Sunset carnival, Jack in Pulpit. Fine Cut and Grapes pattern. Limited Edition, Mini Collection. Distributed by LeVay, made by Fenton Art Glass Company.

608. 6" Red Sunset carnival vase. Called Handkerchief vase. Fine Cut and Grapes. Made by Fenton.

609. 4" Red Sunset carnival spittoon. Fine Cut and Grapes. Made by Fenton.

610. 4" Red Sunset carnival cupped rosebowl. 3-footed with Fine Cut and Grapes. Made by Fenton.

611. 8½" Red Sunset carnival basket. Fine Cut and grapes with looped handle double crimped. Limited Edition with 1000 of each in series. Made by Fenton.

612. 7¼" carnival turkey. Made by L.E. Smith.

613. 9" satin hat. Red satin outside and white satin inside. Signed and dated. Numbered Limited Edition. Made at Fenton in 1985.

614. 10" satin basket with ruby satin outside, white satin inside and clear handle. Numbered, signed and dated on the bottom. Made by Fenton Art Glass in 1985.

615. 18¼" satin cane with ruby and white candy stripes. Made by Fenton in 1985.

616. 7" owl bank bought in 81 in Indiana. Made by Anchor Hocking in 1981; Marked Anchor Hocking on bottom.

617. 4x7½ elephant candy dish with lid. Made about 1927.

618. 11¼" Alley Cat door stop. Made with a mould purchased from the United States Glass Company. Originally designed by Reuben Haley for Duncan and Miller. Made by Fenton in 1984.

619. 3" Mirror Images' small bear. Reproduction from old New Martinsville molds. Limited editions. Made by Viking Glass in 1986.

620. 6" Robin covered candy dish. Made by Westmoreland in 1980.

621. 8" Rearing Horse bookends Made by L.E. Smith in 1981.

622. 5" Robin. Made by Westmoreland from 1979 through 1983.

623. 3¾" whale. Made by Pilgrim in 1982.

624. 4" Oscar donkey. Made for Heisey Collectors of America Inc., in 1985.

625. 3" bird. Bought from Arnold Larson's Gifts, 1980 catalog. Made by Swedish Glass in 1980.

626. 2⅛" medium bird. Same as 625. Made by Swedish Glass in 1980.

627. 8½" bird frog. Made by Viking Glass from 1981 through 1982.

628. 3¼" hand painted fawn. Made by Fenton in 1985.

629. Mirror Images' bear. Made by Viking Glass in 1985 using an old New Martinsville mold.

630. 4½" Mirror Images' seal. Made by Viking Glass in 1985 in ruby, carnival, and satin.

631. 5" Mirror Images' police dog. Limited Edition. Made by Viking Glass from an old New Martinsville mold.

632. 5" elephant. Made by Swedish Glass. Same as 625 and 626.

633. 4½" owl by Mosser, made in 1982.

634. 4" bird. Made by Swedish Glass in 1980. Same as 632.

635. 4½" Fenton butterfly.

636. 4½" pig. Made by Swedish Glass in 1980. Same as 625.

637. 1" mini bird. Made by Swedish Glass in 1980. Same as 625.

638. 1" piglets. Made by Imperial from Heisey molds through the 1960s.

639. Medium bird. Made by Swedish Glass in 1980. Same as 625.

Fenton Inventory, Ruby Glass Entries
(See explanation on page x)

Description of items		Inventory Value	Reference
1914			
1 bbl. 1 doz. 180 Ruby Lemo. set		5.50	
#509-510 Vases - Ruby 30 doz.		34.50	[Fig. 94; Heacock, Fenton 1, p.102]
#1 Ruby Tumbler - Plain 130 doz.		18.00	
#59 Jug - Ruby Plain 15 doz.		52.50	
#1829 Dec. Jug - Ruby 7 doz.		28.00	[Heacock, Fenton 1, p. 63?]
1915			
4 doz. 517 Vase - Ruby	2.50	10.00	[Heacock, Fenton 1, pp. 25, 104]
200 doz. E. Sign Caps - Ruby	.48	96.00	
1918			
200 doz. 597 Ruby Tumblers		176.00	
16 doz. 1 Sign Cap - Ruby		12.00	
14 doz. 16 Sign Cap - Ruby		31.50	
50 doz. 4 Op Sign Cap - Ruby		37.50	
50 doz. 4 Op Cap - Ruby		37.50	
20 doz. Red Lantern Globes		38.00	
1920			
100 doz. 597 Ruby Tumblers		93.00	
1921			
35 doz. 603 Crimp Bwl. - Blue, Pearl, Gr. & Ruby		336.00	[Heacock, Fenton 1, pp. 87, 91]
4 doz. 9 Candy Jar - Ruby		25.60	[Heacock, Fenton 1, pp. 86, 91]
11 doz. 8 Candy Jar - Ruby		59.39	[Heacock, Fenton 1, pp. 86, 91]

Fenton Inventory, Ruby Glass Entries *(continued)*

Description of items	Inventory Value	Reference
27 doz. 604-12" Fld. Bowl - Ruby, Gold, Blue & Green	583.20	[Heacock, Fenton 1, p. 87]
14 doz. 604-14" Shal. & Fld Cup Gold [,] Ruby Green & Blue	302.40	[Heacock, Fenton 1, p. 87]
122 doz. 103 Sherbet Gr Gold [,] Ruby Yellow Topaz & Wisteria	234.24	[Heacock, Fenton 1, pp. 86, 90]
198 doz. 2006 Cup & Shallow Pr. Gold [,] Ruby & Green	871.20	[Heacock, Fenton 1, pp. 87, 89]
87-1/2 doz. 647 R. R. D. Cup, Salver & Ftd. Gr. Blue Pr. & Ruby	805.00	[Heacock, Fenton 1, p.88]
149 doz. 2007 Plate Cup & Shal. Gr. Pr. Gold [,] Ruby & Blue	953.60	[Heacock, Fenton 1, pp. 87, 89]
3 doz. #2 F. Block Ruby	6.60	
42 doz. 606 Cup Shallow Green & Ruby	218.40	[Heacock, Fenton 1, p. 89]
80 doz. 606 Cup Shallow Gold [,] Ruby, Blue & Pearl		[Heacock, Fenton 1, p.86]
11 doz. 349 - 10" C. Stick - Wisteria & Ruby	416.00	[Heacock, Fenton 1, p. 89]
11 doz. 249 C. Stick - Ruby	145.64	[Heacock, Fenton 1, pp. 86, 88]
72-1/2 doz. 600-7-10" Cup & Shal. - Pearl, Blue & Ruby	88.00	[Heacock, Fenton 1, p.86]
48-1/2 doz. 600-7-10" Cup Shal. - Ruby, Gold & Green	495.90	[Heacock, Fenton 1, p.87?]
90 doz. 607 Cup & Shallow Gr. Gold [,] Ruby, Blue & Pearl	323.66	[Heacock, Fenton 1, p.87?]
31 doz. 602 Van. - Pearl, Green, Blue & Ruby	594.00	[Heacock, Fenton 1, pp.86. 87, 89]
	297.60	[Heacock, Fenton 1, pp. 88, 90?]

Fenton Inventory, Ruby Glass Entries *(continued)*

Description of items	Inventory Value	Reference
90 doz. 109 Cup - Ruby, Blue & Green 1923	172.80	[Heacock, Fenton 1, pp. 87, 89 (different shape)]
126 doz. 598 Ruby Tumblers 1924	90.72	
14 doz. 607 Bowl - Orange, Ruby, J Yellow	89.60	[Heacock, Fenton 1, 86, 87, 89]
3 doz. 736 Candy Jar - Ruby	26.40	[Heacock, Fenton 1, p.86]
3 doz. 8 Candy Jar - Ruby	20.16	[Heacock, Fenton 1, pp. 86, 91]
3 doz. 9 Candy Jar - Ruby	24.00	[Heacock, Fenton 1, pp. 86, 91]
5 doz. 643 Salver - C Yellow & Ruby	17.60	[Heacock, Fenton 1, pp. 86, 91, 92]
5 doz. 647 Bowl - Orange & Ruby	50.00	[Heacock, Fenton 1, pp. 86, 88; Heacock, Fenton 2, p. 87]
3 doz. 449 Candlestick - Ruby & C Yellow	18.00	[Heacock, Fenton 1, pp. 86, 90, 93]
7 doz. 549 Candlestick - Ruby & C yellow	64.40	[Frank M. Fenton, "Fenton Coasters", Butterfly Net, January 1984, p.6]
5 doz. 649 Candlestick - Yellow & Ruby	66.00	[Frank M. Fenton, "Fenton Coasters", Butterfly Net, January 1984, p.6]
1 doz. 55 Cologne - Ruby	7.20	[Heacock, Fenton 1, p.62]
253 doz. 598 Fld. - Ruby	182.16	
43 doz. 595-24 Fld. - Ruby	45.15	
3-3/4 doz. 50 Fld. - Ruby	4.69	
159 doz. 596-10 hr. Fld. - Ruby	106.51	
40 doz. 999 Wine - Ruby	24.00	
5/6 doz. 549 Candlestick - Ruby & Crystal	19.16	[Frank M. Fenton, "Fenton Coasters", Butterfly Net, January 1984, p.6]
3/4 doz. 604 Plate - Irid. Ruby	31.50	

Fenton Inventory, Ruby Glass Entries *(continued)*

Description of items	Inventory Value	Reference
1/6 doz. 647-10 Fld. Bowl and Base - Plain Ruby	5.42	[Heacock, Fenton 1, p.88]
1/3 doz. 647 Plate and Base - pl. Ruby	10.83	
1/3 doz. 647 Shl. R. Rim Bowl & Base - pl. Ruby	10.83	[Heacock, Fenton 1, p.88?]
1/3 doz. 2007 Plate - Irid. Ruby	7.07	
3-1/3 doz. 2007 Ftd. Nappy - Irid. Ruby	33.33	
7/12 doz. 2006 Plate - Irid. Ruby	8.75	
1-1/12 doz. 2006 Shl. Bowl and Base - Irid. Ruby	20.85	
1-1/12 doz. 2007 Shl. Bowl and Base - Irid. Ruby	23.75	[Heacock, Fenton 1, pp. 87?, 89?, 91?]
1/2 doz. 604 Crimped Bowl - Irid. Ruby	36.00	[Heacock, Fenton 2, p. 62]
2-7/12 doz. 2006 Oval - Irid. Bury [Ruby?]	50.66	
3/4 doz. 601 Shal. Bowl & Base - Irid. Bury [Ruby?]	15.75	[Heacock, Fenton 1, p.87]
1/3 doz. 604/Fld. Bowl & Base - Irid. Ruby	25.00	[Heacock, Fenton 1, p.87]
2-1/6 doz. 602 Vase & Bowl - Irid. Ruby	81.14	[Heacock, Fenton 1, pp. 88, 90]
3 doz. 100 Tulip Comport - Ruby	14.40	
14 doz. 607 Roll Rim - P Ruby, & C Yellow	89.60	[Heacock, Fenton 1, p. 87]
3 doz. 647-12" Ftd. - P Ruby	30.00	
8 doz. 647 Fld. Salver - P Ruby, & C Yellow	80.00	
3-1/2 doz. 749 Candlestick - P Ruby	70.00	[Frank M. Fenton, "Fenton Coasters", Butterfly Net, January, 1984, p.6]
[?]-2/3 doz. 603 Cup Orange Bowl - Irid. Ruby & Plain Ruby	48.40	
[?] 4 doz. 2005 Mayon Bowl - Plain Ruby	72.80	[Heacock, Fenton 1, p.87]
30 doz. 103 Plate - Plain Ruby, C Yellow	72.00	[Heacock, Fenton 1, p.87]
2 doz. 1006 Cup - Irid. Ruby	10.00	[Heacock, Fenton 1, pp. 86, 90]

Fenton Inventory, Ruby Glass Entries *(continued)*

Description of items	Inventory Value	Reference
3 doz. 1006 Plate - Irid. Ruby	15.00	[Heacock, Fenton 1, pp. 87, 89]
15 doz. 109 Mayon Plate - Plain Ruby	36.00	
22 doz. 109 Cup - Irid. Ruby & Plain Ruby	88.00	
2-1/2 doz. 600 Salad - Irid. Ruby & Orange	21.00	[Heacock, Fenton 1, pp. 87, 89]
10 doz. 600 Salver - Plain Ruby, C Yellow	67.20	
5 doz. 349 Candlestick - Irid. Ruby	54.00	[Heacock, Fenton 1, pp. 86, 88]
2-1/2 doz. 449 Candlestick - Irid. Ruby	150.00	[Heacock, Fenton 1, pp. 86, 90, 93]
1-1/2 doz. 604 F Cup - Irid. Ruby	48.00	[Heacock, Fenton 1, P.87]
3 doz. 607 Plate - Irid. Ruby	19.20	
1-1/4 doz. 602 Fld. Vase - Irid. Ruby	225.00	[Heacock, Fenton 1, pp. 88, 90]
4 doz. 250 F Dish - Plain Ruby	29.00	[Heacock, Fenton 1, p. 86]
1925		
2/3 doz 249 Candlestick - Plain Ruby	2.67	[Heacock, Fenton 1, p.86; Heacock, Fenton 2, p.93]
5-3/4 doz. 349 Candlestick - Plain Ruby	14.50	[Heacock, Fenton 1, pp. 86, 88]
24 doz. 549 Candlestick- Ven-Red, Ruby & Chin-Yellow	144.00	[Frank M. Fenton, "Fenton Coasters", Butterfly Net, January 1984, p. 6]
12-1/4 doz. 449 Candlestick - Ruby & Ven Red	62.50	[Heacock, Fenton 1, pp. 86, 90, 93]
50 doz. 314 Candlestick - Ruby & Chin-Yellow	135.00	[Heacock, Fenton 1, p. 93]
12 doz. 232 Candlestick - Ruby & Orange	74.00	[Heacock, Fenton 1, p. 90]
14 doz. 56 Cologne - Plain [sic] Ruby	100.80	[Weatherman, Colored Glassware 2, p. 102]
8 doz. 55 Cologne - Ruby	57.60	[Heacock, Fenton 1, p. 62]
1-1/2 doz. 561 Fan Vase - Ruby	6.36	
1-1/2 doz. 560 Fan Vase - Ruby	5.40	

Fenton Inventory, Ruby Glass Entries *(continued)*

Description of items	Inventory Value	Reference
11-1/2 doz. 612 Vase - Ruby & Chin-Yellow	60.75	[Heacock, Fenton 1, p. 90]
4 doz. 602 Fld. Vase - Ruby	41.60	[Heacock, Fenton 1, pp. 88, 90]
20 doz. 622 Vase - Plain Ruby	160.00	[Frank M. Fenton, "Fenton Coasters", Butterfly Net, January 1984, p.6]
9 doz. 611 Vase - Ruby & Chin-yellow	50.40	[Frank M. Fenton, "Fenton Coasters", Butterfly Net, January 1984, p.6]
1-1/3 doz. 621 Ruby Vase	10.67	[Heacock, Fenton 2, pp. 66-68, 92-94]
110 doz. 251 Bud Vase - Ruby, Orange & Ven-Red	550.00	[Heacock, Fenton 1, pp. 86, 91]
5 doz. 316 Sherbet - Plain Ruby & Chin-Yellow	12.00	
12 doz. 403 Sherbet - Plain Ruby	28.80	[Weatherman, Colored Glassware 2, p. 102]
24 doz. 543 Bon-Bon - Ruby & Chin-Yellow [hand written: 643 Bon-Bon Chin-Yellow, Ruby]	120.00	[543: Heacock, Fenton 1, p. 91. 643: Heacock, Fenton 1, pp. 86, 90, 93]
15 doz. 57 Puff Box - Plain Ruby	64.00	[Weatherman, Colored Glassware 2, p. 102]
7 doz. 743 Puff Box - Plain Ruby	35.00	[Frank M. Fenton, "Fenton Coasters", Butterfly Net, January 1984, p.6]
9 doz. 9 Candy Jar - Plain Ruby	59.40	[Heacock, Fenton 1, pp. 86, 91]
8 doz. 8 Candy Jar - Plain Ruby	40.00	[Heacock, Fenton 1, pp. 86, 91]
8 doz. 736 Candy Jar - Plain Ruby & Chin-Yellow	57.60	[Heacock, Fenton 1, p. 86]
5 doz. 635 Candy Jar - Plain Ruby	25.00	[Weatherman, Colored Glassware 2, p.102]
10 doz. 735 Candy Jar - Ruby	50.00	[Heacock, Fenton 1, pp. 90, 93]
74-1/4 doz. 636 Candy Jar - Ven-Red, Ruby & Chin-Yellow	536.40	[Heacock, Fenton 1, pp. 66, 86]
5 doz. 737 Comport - Plain Ruby	30.00	[Frank M. Fenton, "Fenton Coasters", Butterfly Net, January 1984, p. 6]

Fenton Inventory, Ruby Glass Entries (*continued*)

Description of items	Inventory Value	Reference
4 doz. 316 Comport - Plain Ruby	26.40	[Heacock, Fenton 1, p. 73]
1 doz. 260 Comport - Ruby	6.80	[Heacock, Fenton 1, p. 86]
5 doz. 250 Fern Bowl - Plain Ruby	37.00	[Heacock, Fenton 1, p. 90: Heacock, Fenton 2, pp. 67, 68, 93, 94, 97]
20-1/2 doz. 846 Asstd Shapes - Ruby	118.90	[Heacock, Fenton 1, pp. 87, 89; Heacock, Fenton 2, p.87]
18-1/4 doz. 600 Asstd Shapes - Ruby	125.80	
19 doz. 607 Asstd Shapes - Ven-Red, Chin-Yellow & Ruby	98.80	[Heacock, Fenton 1, pp. 86, 87, 89]
5 doz. 550 Asstd Shapes - Ruby	45.00	[Heacock, Fenton 1, pp. 86, 87, 90, 93]
32-1/2 doz. 640 Asstd Shapes - Ruby, Chin-Yellow & Ven-Red	162.50	[Heacock, Fenton 1, pp. 87, 89, 90]
33 doz. 647 Asstd Shapes - Ruby, Chin-Yellow & Ven-Red	283.80	[Heacock, Fenton 1, pp. 86, 88; Heacock, Fenton 2, p.87]
1-1/4 doz. 603 Orange Bowl - Ruby	16.40	[Heacock, Fenton 1, pp. 87, 91]
9-1/2 doz. 638 Asstd Shapes - Ruby, Chin-Yellow & Ven-Red	46.60	[Heacock, Fenton 1, pp. 87, 89]
39 doz. 643 Asstd Shapes - Ruby & Chin-Yellow & Ven-Red	137.26	[Heacock, Fenton 1, pp. 86, 90-93]
186 doz. 547 Bowl - Asstd Colors [hand written: 109-Asst. Shapes, Ruby & Chin-Yellow	535.88	[109: Heacock, Fenton 1, pp. 87, 89]
25 doz. 3" Flower Block - Ruby & Chin-Yellow	45.00	[Heacock, Fenton 1, p. 86?]

Fenton Inventory, Ruby Glass Entries *(continued)*

Description of items	Inventory Value	Reference
92 doz. 2" Flower Block - Ruby, Orange & Chin-Yellow	110.40	[Heacock, Fenton 1, p. 86?]
18 doz. 312 Asstd Shapes - Ruby	72.00	[Frank M. Fenton, "Fenton Coasters", Butterfly Net, January 1984, p.6]
21 doz. 758 Plate - Ruby	84.00	[Frank M. Fenton, "Fenton Coasters", Butterfly Net, January 1984, p.6]
12 doz. 681 Plate - Ruby	98.00	[Frank M. Fenton, "Fenton Coasters", Butterfly Net, January 1984, p.6]
26 doz. 630 Plate - Orange, Chin-yellow & Ruby	146.00	[Heacock, Fenton 1, pp. 86, 87]
1/2 doz. 918 Bowl - Ruby	6.00	
28-1/2 doz. 231 Asstd Shapes - Ruby & Orange	171.00	[Heacock, Fenton 1, p. 90; Heacock, Fenton 2, pp. 94, 97, 98]
4 doz. 317 Sand & Nut Tray - Ruby	36.00	[Frank M. Fenton, "Fenton Coasters", Butterfly Net, January 1984, p.6; Heacock, Fenton 1, p.66]
12 doz. 679 Plate - Ruby	39.60	[Heacock, Fenton 1, pp. 86, 90}
18 doz. 103 Plate - Ruby	43.80	[Heacock, Fenton 1, pp. 87, 89; Heacock, Fenton 2, p.62]
12-3/4 doz. 604 Nappy - Ruby	387.60	
88 doz. 598 Tumbler - Ruby	63.36	
23 doz. 596 Tumbler - Ruby	16.56	
30 doz. 599 Tumbler - Ruby	31.50	[Heacock, Fenton 1, p.94?]
1926		
4 doz. 682 Plate - Ruby	50.00	[Frank M. Fenton, "Fenton Coasters", Butterfly Net, January 1984, p. 6;

Fenton Inventory, Ruby Glass Entries (*continued*)

Description of items		Inventory Value	Reference
14 doz. 562 Vase - Ruby		252.00	[Heacock, Fenton 1, p. 93]
105 doz. Blown Ruby Candle - Small		630.00	
2 doz. 749 Candlestick - Ruby		80.00	[Frank M. Fenton, "Fenton Coasters", Butterfly Net, January 1984, p.6]
30 doz. 201 Coaster - Ruby		45.00	
16 doz. 1 Base - Black, Ruby & Topaz		64.00	
28 doz. 8 Day Ruby Candle		182.00	
76 doz. Ruby & Green Glass	Diamond Candle Co.	200.16	
50 doz. #1 Sign Cap, Ruby 1927	Reynolds Elec. Co.	280.00	
18 doz. 680 Plate - Ruby		108.00	[Frank M. Fenton, "Fenton Coasters", Butterfly Net, January 1984, p. 6; Heacock, Fenton 2, pp. 112, 116, 117]
3 doz. 681 Plate - Ruby		30.00	[Frank M. Fenton, "Fenton Coasters", Butterfly Net, January 1984, p. 6]
84 doz. 1126 Vase - Ruby		88.20	[Heacock, Fenton 1, pp. 83, 94, 113]
8 doz. 916 Vase - Ruby		16.00	[Heacock, Fenton 1, pp. 83, 104]
100 doz. 912 Vase - Ruby 1929		160.00	
Cartons 12 doz. ea Tumblers - Ruby		748.00	
Cartons 6 doz. ea Tumblers - Ruby 1930		336.00	
15 doz. 1635 Tumblers [sic]		60.00	[Heacock, Fenton 1, p. 110]

Fenton Inventory, Ruby Glass Entries (*continued*)

Description of items	Inventory Value	Reference
1931		
145 doz. 1611 Goblet-Black, Jade, Ruby & Royal Blue	253.75	[Fig. 105]
10 doz. 1611 Ftd. Tumblers - Black, Jade, Ruby & Royal Blue	17.50	[Heacock, Fenton 2, p. 82]
70 doz. 1611 Clarets - Black, Jade, Ruby & Royal Blue	115.50	[Heacock, Fenton 2, p. 82]
60 doz. 1611 Cocktails - Black, Jade Ruby & Royal Blue	90.00	[Heacock, Fenton 2, p. 82]
15 doz. 1611 Finger Bowls - Black, Jade, Ruby & Royal Blue	33.75	[Heacock, Fenton 2, p. 82]
20 doz. 1611 Jugs - Black, Jade, Ruby & Royal Blue	180.00	[Fig. 102]
100 doz. 1611 Sugar & Cream Sets - Black, Jade, Ruby & Royal Blue	400.00	[Fig. 103]
100 doz. 1611 Cups & Saucers - Black, Jade, Ruby & Royal Blue	300.00	[Heacock, Fenton 2, p. 82]
115 doz. 1611 Whiskey - Black, Jade, Ruby & Royal Blue	109.25	[Heacock, Fenton 2, p. 82]
220 doz. 1611 Low Sherbet - Black, Jade, Ruby & Royal Blue	135.00	[Fig. 97; Heacock, Fenton 2, p. 82]
100 doz. 1611 9 oz. Tumbler - Black, Jade, Ruby & Royal Blue	100.00	[Heacock, Fenton 2, p. 82]
100 doz. 1611 5 oz. Tumbler - Black Jade Ruby & Royal Blue	95.00	[Heacock, Fenton 2, p. 82]

Fenton Inventory, Ruby Glass Entries (*continued*)

Description of items	Inventory Value	Reference
80 doz. 1611 Ice Tea - Black, Jade, Ruby & Royal Blue	120.00	[Heacock, Fenton 2, p. 82]
50 doz. 1611 Hi Ftd. Sherbet - Black, Jade, Ruby & Royal Blue	87.50	[Fig. 104]
60 doz. 1611 Nut Cups - Black, Jade, Ruby & Royal Blue	60.00	[Heacock, Fenton 2, p. 82]
35 doz. 1611 Cordials - Black, Jade, Ruby & Royal Blue	35.00	[Heacock, Fenton 2, p. 82]
25 doz. 1611 Candlesticks - Black, Jade & Ruby	75.00	["Recent Discoveries", Butterfly Net, January 1982, p.8]
14 doz. 1611 8" Bowl - Black, Jade, Ruby & Royal Blue	105.00	
30 doz. 1611 Decanters - Black, Jade, Ruby & Royal Blue	225.00	[Fig. 96; Heacock, Fenton 2, p. 30]
60 doz. 1611 Plates - Black, Jade, Ruby & Royal Blue	135.00	[Heacock, Fenton 2, p. 82]
50 doz. 1611 8" Plates - Black, Jade, Ruby & Royal Blue	125.00	[Fig. 107]
25 doz. 1700 Cups & Saucers - Jade, Black, Ruby & Royal Blue	112.50	[Figs. 117, 118]
22 doz. 1700 Sherbet - Jade, Black, Ruby & Royal Blue	60.50	[Fig. 120]
25 doz. 1700 Goblet - Jade, Black, Ruby & Royal Blue	68.75	[Fig. 122]

Fenton Inventory, Ruby Glass Entries (*continued*)

Description of items	Inventory Value	Reference
25 doz. 1700 Sugar & Cream Sets - Black, Jade, Ruby & Royal Blue	187.50	[Fig. 125]
5 doz. 1700 Ice Teas - Black, Jade, Ruby & Royal Blue	15.00	[Heacock, Fenton 1, p. 108]
13 doz. 1700 Finger Bowls & Plates - Black, Jade, Ruby & Royal Blue	78.00	[Finger bowl: Fig. 118. Finger bowl and plate: Heacock, Fenton 1, p. 108]
5 doz. 1700 Tumbler - Black, Jade, Ruby & Royal Blue	13.75	[Heacock, Fenton 1, p. 108]
7 doz. 1700 Wine - Black, Jade, Ruby & Royal Blue	15.40	[See Fig. 121 text]
18 doz. 1700 Cocktail - Black, Jade, Ruby & Royal Blue	45.00	[See Fig. 121 text]
1932		
30 doz. 1700-12 oz. Ice Teas, Ruby	90.00	[Heacock, Fenton 1, p. 108]
32 doz. 1700 Cocktails, Royal Blue, Ruby	80.00	[See Fig. 121 text]
21 doz. 1636 Ice Teas - Royal Blue, Ruby	42.00	[Heacock, Fenton 1, p.110]
12 doz. 519 Vases - Ruby, Royal Blue	108.00	
50 doz. 1504-A Bowls - Ruby, Royal Blue & Yellow	225.00	[Heacock, Fenton 1, pp. 92, 110; Heacock, Fenton 2, p.87]
10 doz. 1639 - 8" Plates - Ruby	25.00	[Heacock, Fenton 2, p. 65?]
10 doz. 1502 - 8" Vases - Ruby	60.00	[Heacock, Fenton 1, pp. 93?, 110?, 111?]
15 doz. 1639 - 12" Hdld Plates - Ruby, Jade	90.00	[Heacock, Fenton 2, p. 87]
15 doz. 183 - 10" Vases - Ruby	90.00	[Heacock, Fenton 2, pp. 70, 91]

Fenton Inventory, Ruby Glass Entries (*continued*)

Description of items	Inventory Value	Reference
330 doz. 1590 Coasters - Ruby, Jade, Black, R. Blue & Moonstone	330.00	[Frank Fenton, "Fenton Coasters", Butterfly Net, March 1984, pp. 5, 6]
35 doz. 847 - 6" Nap. Jade & Ruby	115.50	[Heacock, Fenton 2, pp. 67, 68, 92; Heacock, Fenton 1, p. 93]
110 doz. 857 - 7" Nap. Ruby, Black and Jade	726.00	[Heacock, Fenton 1, p.88?]
40 doz. 1611 Salt & Pepper Sets - Blue, Ruby	240.00	[Fig. 106]
6 doz. 1611 - 12" Grill Plates - Ruby, Royal Blue	27.00	[Fig. 473?]
28 doz. 1611 Jugs - Ruby, Blue & Black	252.00	
10 doz. 1611 Jugs - Ice Lip - Ruby	90.00	[Fig. 102]
6 doz. 1611 C. Sticks - Ruby	18.00	["Recent Discoveries", Butterfly Net, January 1982, p. 8]
4 doz. 1611 Candy Jar - Ruby	30.00	[Belknap, p. 235?]
30 doz. 1611 Cordial - Ruby	30.00	[Heacock, Fenton 2, p. 82]
14 doz. 1611 Nut Dish - Ruby, Royal Blue	14.00	[Heacock, Fenton 2, p. 82]
[?] 05 doz. 1611-2-3/4 oz. Tumblers - Royal Blue, Ruby, Topaz, Jade & Black	194.75	[Heacock, Fenton 2, p. 82]
205 doz. 1611 - 5 oz. Tumblers - Royal Blue Ruby & Topaz	194.75	[Heacock, Fenton 2, p. 82]
58 doz. 1611 Sugar - Jade, Ruby, Black & Topaz	116.00	[Fig. 103]
65 doz. 1611 Creamers - Jade, Ruby, Black, Topaz, Royal Blue	130.00	[Fig. 103]
56 doz. 1611 Saucers - Ruby, Black, R. Blue	84.00	[Heacock, Fenton 2, p. 82]
3 doz. 1611 Cocktail Shakers - Ruby	72.00	[Heacock, Fenton 2, p. 82]

Fenton Inventory, Ruby Glass Entries *(continued)*

Description of items	Inventory Value	Reference
15 doz. 1611 Oval Bon-Bons - Ruby, Blue	15.00	["More Georgian?", National Duncan Glass Journal, July-September, 1987, fourth page of article?]
10 doz. 1611 Salver - Ruby	10.00	
58 doz. 1611 Hi Ftd. Sherbet - Ruby, Royal Blue	101.50	[Fig. 104]
43 doz. 1611 Cocktails - Ruby, R. Blue	64.53	[Heacock, Fenton 2, p. 82]
65 doz. 1611 - 4-1/2 oz. Claret - Ruby, Royal Blue	107.25	[Heacock, Fenton 2, p. 82]
5 doz. 1611 - 8" Nap. - Cup & Fld - Ruby	22.50	
103 doz. 1611 - 12 oz. Ice Teas - Royal Blue, Ruby & Black	154.50	[Heacock, Fenton 2, p. 82]
150 doz. 1611 Goblets - Royal Blue, Ruby, Black	262.50	[Fig. 105]
85 doz. 1611 - 9 oz. Ftd. Tumblers - R. Blue, Ruby, Black	148.75	[Heacock, Fenton 2, p. 82]
10 doz. 1611 Finger Bowls - Ruby	22.50	[Heacock, Fenton 2, p. 82]
125 doz. 107 Vases - Asstd - Ruby, Jade & Royal Blue	200.00	[Heacock, Fenton 2, p. 96]
40 doz. 600 Nappy - Ruby, Royal Blue	240.00	[Heacock, Fenton 1, pp. 87, 89; Heacock, Fenton 2, p.87]
25 doz. 1611 Vase - Ruby, Royal Blue	150.00	["More Georgian?", National Duncan Glass Journal, July-September, 1987, fourth page of article?]
1933		
78 doz. 1620 Goblet - Ruby	130.50	[Heacock, Fenton 2, p. 30]
15 doz. 1620 Sherbet - Ruby	26.25	[Fig. 89]
36 doz. 1620 Wines - Ruby	50.40	[Heacock, Fenton 2, p. 83]
6 doz. 1620 - 8" Plate - Ruby	18.00	[Weatherman, Colored Glassware 2, p. 105, lower (9 oz.?)]

Fenton Inventory, Ruby Glass Entries *(continued)*

Description of items	Inventory Value	Reference
6 doz. 1620 - 9 oz. Tumblers - Ruby	7.50	[Weatherman, Colored Glassware 2, p.105, lower (9 oz.?)]
20 doz. 1620 Ice Teas - Ruby	34.00	[Heacock, Fenton 2, p. 30?]
5 doz. 1620 Hi Ball - Ruby	6.75	[Heacock, Fenton 2, p. 83]
16 doz. 1620 - 5 oz. Tumbler Ruby	18.40	[Weatherman, Colored Glassware 2, p. 105, lower (5 oz.?)
6 doz. 1620 Pilsner - Ruby	10.50	[Heacock, Fenton 2, p. 83]
80 doz. 1611 Salts - Ruby, Blue	240.00	[Fig. 106]
20 doz. 1611 - 8 oz. Mug - Ruby	40.00	[Gwen Shumpert, "Gwen's Glassline", Glass Review, July, 1980, p.10?]
20 doz. 1611 - 12 oz. Mug - Ruby	50.00	
100 doz. 1611 - 9 oz. Tumblers - Ruby	110.00	[Heacock, Fenton 2, p. 82]
19 doz. 1611 Cups - Blue, Ruby	28.50	[Heacock, Fenton 2, p. 82]
22 doz. 1611 Nut Dish - Ruby	22.00	[Heacock, Fenton 2, p. 82]
16 doz. 1611 Cordials - Ruby	16.00	[Heacock, Fenton 2, p. 82]
140 doz. 1611 - 5 oz. Tumblers - Ruby	154.00	[Heacock, Fenton 2, p. 82]
18 doz. 1611 Whiskies - Ruby	19.80	[Heacock, Fenton 2, p. 82]
148 doz. 1611 Cupd Sherbet - Black, Ruby, Royal Blue	162.80	[Fig.97]
74 doz. 1611 Flared Sherbet - Royal Blue, Ruby	81.40	
173 doz. 1611 Sugar, Cream - Jade, Topaz, Black & Ruby	346.00	[Fig. 103]
55 doz. 1611 Candlesticks - Ruby, Blue & Milk	165.00	["Recent Discoveries", Butterfly Net, January 1982, p. 8]
113 doz. 1611 4-1/2 oz. Claret - Blue, Ruby	186.46	[Heacock, Fenton 2, p. 82]
38 doz. 1611 Cocktail - Ruby, Royal Blue	57.00	[Heacock, Fenton 2, p. 82]

Fenton Inventory, Ruby Glass Entries *(continued)*

Description of items	Inventory Value	Reference
76 doz. 1611 Goblet - Milk, Ruby & Blue	133.00	[Fig. 105]
57 doz. 1611 Footed Tumbler - Black, Royal Blue, Ruby	99.75	[Heacock, Fenton 2, p. 82]
61 doz. 1611 - 9" Cupd Bowl - Ruby, Royal Blue & Milk	457.50	[Heacock, Fenton 2, p. 82]
50 doz. 1611 Finger Bowls - Ruby, Blue	112.50	[Fig. 102]
8 doz. 1611 Jugs - Ruby	72.00	["More Georgian?", National Duncan Glass Journal, July-September, 1987, fourth page of article?]
35 doz. 1611 Bon-Bons - 5" Blue, Ruby	38.50	
161 doz. 1611 - 8" Plates - Royal Blue, Black & Ruby	402.50	[Fig. 107]
30 doz. 1611 - 6" Plates - Royal Blue, Black & Ruby	67.50	[Heacock, Fenton 2, p. 82]
300 doz. 1611 & 1639-6" Plates, Ruby, Black, Blue	600.00	[1611: Heacock, Fenton 2, p. 82. 1639: Heacock, Fenton 2, p. 65
36 doz. 1611 - 10" Plates - Blue, Ruby	126.00	[Eddie Unger, "Comparison of Fenton vs Duncan & Miller Georgian", National Duncan Glass Journal, April-June, 1987, p.17; Edie Unger, "'Georgian' Controversy", Glass Review, November, 1987, p. 2]
61 doz. 1611 Hi Ftd. Sherbet - Milk, Ruby & Blue	106.75	[Fig. 104]
14 doz. 2010 - 10 oz. Mug - Ruby	35.00	
72 doz. 621 Vase - Ruby, P. Blue, C. Yellow, Jade, Moon	345.00	[Heacock, Fenton 2, pp. 66-68, 92-94]
36 doz. 1932 - 5" Cr. Nap - Ruby	29.16	[Heacock, Fenton 1, p.113?]
10 doz. 185 - 6" Cr. Vase - Ruby	45.00	[Heacock, Fenton 2, p. 87]
3 doz. 1237 - 10" Cr. Bowl - Ruby	18.00	[Heacock, Fenton 2, p. 66 (different shape)]

Fenton Inventory, Ruby Glass Entries (continued)

Description of items	Inventory Value	Reference
213 doz. 1643 Flower Block - Moon, Black, Milk, Crystal, Ruby, P. Blue, Jade, D. Gr, L. Gr, & Royal Blue	372.75	[Fig. 99?]
7 doz. 184-12" Vase - G. O., Ruby	52.50	[Heacock, Fenton 2, pp. 81, 87, 92, 93]
6 doz. 519-20" Vase - Ruby	225.00	
19 doz. 519-20" Vase - Black	234.00	
26 doz. 1700-14" Plate - Ruby, Blue		
25 doz. 1639 Sherbet Ruby	62.50	[Heacock, Fenton 2, p. 65]
82 doz. 857 Bowls - Asstd Shapes - Jade, Ruby & Black	541.20	[Heacock, Fenton 1, pp. 88, 92, 93; Heacock, Fenton 2, pp. 66, 87, 92]
170-1/2 doz. 848 Bowls - Fld & Cupd - Ruby, Moon, C. Yellow, Rose, Blue, Black, Lilac, Jade & P. Blue	852.50	[Fig. 100; Heacock, Fenton 2, p. 64]
539 doz. 848 Candlesticks - Ruby, Jade	436.59	[Fig. 101]
59 doz. 847 Bowls Asstd Shapes - Jade, Ruby	194.70	[Heacock, Fenton 1, pp. 90-93, 110; Heacock, Fenton 2, pp. 66-68, 92]
157 doz. 1590 Coasters - Moonstone, Jade, Black & Ruby	157.00	[Frank Fenton, "Fenton Coasters", Butterfly Net, March 1984, pp. 5, 6]
25 doz. 49 Tumblers, Ruby	25.00	
22 doz. 1616 Ice pack - Ruby, R. Blue	198.00	[Heacock, Fenton 1, pp. 93, 110; Heacock, Fenton 2, pp. 92, 97]
24 doz. 1618 Basket-Ruby, Crystal, P. Blue, Lilac	172.00	[Fig. 116]

Fenton Inventory, Ruby Glass Entries (*continued*)

Description of items	Inventory Value	Reference
11 doz. 1684 Basket - Jade, Black, Ruby	66.00	[Heacock, Fenton 2, pp. 66-68, 93]
8 doz. 1681 Jar - Amber		
9 doz. 1681 Jar - Ruby, Jade	153.00	[Heacock, Fenton 2, p. 26, 28]
15 doz. 1663 - 12" Bowl C. Yellow		
14 doz. 1663 12" Bowl - Jade, Ruby, P. Blue	261.00	[Heacock, Fenton 2, p. 66, 86, 91]
50 doz. 100 - 5" Nap - Ruby	40.50	[Heacock, Fenton 2, p. 36 (different shape)?]
15 doz. 318 C. Stick Black		
21 doz. 318 C. Stick Ruby	108.00	[Heacock, Fenton 1, pp. 88, 92, 110; Heacock, Fenton 2, pp. 66, 87]
10 doz. 183-12" Vase - Ruby	60.00	
35 doz. 31 Cup - Ruby	52.50	
40 doz. 1502 - 9 oz. Bridge Goblet - Ruby	70.00	[Heacock, Fenton 1, p.111]
40 doz. 107 Vase - Ruby	64.00	[Heacock, Fenton 2, p. 96]
100 doz. 1933 Tumbler - Ruby	81.00	[Heacock, Fenton 1, p.113]
30 doz. 1611 Ice Tea - Ruby	45.00	[Heacock, Fenton 2, p. 82]
24 doz. 1645 Nymph - Ruby, Blue, Black, Yellow, L. Blue, L. Gr, Jade, Crystal & Rose	684.75	[Fig. 99]
56 doz. 1639-8" Plate - Ruby, Black	140.00	[Heacock, Fenton 2, p. 65]
160 doz. 598-15 hr Tumbler - Ruby, Blue & Moonstone	112.00	
25 doz. 599 Tumbler - Ruby	25.00	[Heacock, Fenton 1, p. 94?]
5 doz. 184 - 12" Cut Vase - Jade, Ruby, Black, Blue	60.00	[Heacock, Fenton 2, p. 81]
159 doz. 706 Ivy Ball - P.O., F.O., Royal Blue, Black, L. Green, Amber, Rose & Ruby	858.60	

Fenton Inventory, Ruby Glass Entries (*continued*)

Description of items	Inventory Value	Reference
8 doz. 1668 Flip Vase - Irid, Ruby & Amber 1934	48.00	[Heacock, Fenton 2, p. 87]
59 doz. 1620 Goblets-F.O., Amber & Ruby	103.15	[Weatherman, Colored Glassware 2, p.105, lower]
127 doz. 1620 Sherbets F.O., Amber & Ruby	222.14	[Fig. 89]
130 doz. 1620 Wines F.O., Amber & Ruby	214.50	[Heacock, Fenton 2, p. 83]
27 doz. 1620 - 8 oz. Pilsner - F.O. & Ruby	47.23	[Heacock, Fenton 2, p. 83]
72 doz. 1620-5 oz. Tumbler - F.O. Ruby & Amber	82.80	[Weatherman, Colored Glassware 2, p. 105, lower (5 oz.?)]
72 doz. 1620-5 oz. Tumbler - Ruby & Amber	90.00	[Weatherman, Colored Glassware 2, p. 105, lower (9 oz.?)]
15 doz. 1620-12 oz. Ice Tea - Ruby	25.50	[Heacock, Fenton 2, p. 30?]
15 doz. 1620-7 oz. Old Fash. Cocktail-Amber & Ruby	20.25	[Heacock, Fenton 2, p. 83]
36 doz. 1620-8" Plate-Amber & Ruby	108.00	[Weatherman, Colored Glassware 2, p.105, lower (8?)]
33 doz. 1620-6" Plate - Amber & Ruby	82.50	[Heacock, Fenton 2, p. 83]
1-1/2 doz. 1620 Bar Bottle - Ruby	10.80	[Heacock, Fenton 1, p.113?]
75 doz. 1932 - 5" Nappy - Ruby	60.75	[Heacock, Fenton 2, p. 82]
45 doz. 1611 - 9 oz. Tumbler - Ruby	49.50	[Heacock, Fenton 2, p. 82]
23 doz. 1611 - 12 oz. Ice tea - Ruby	34.50	[Heacock, Fenton 2, p. 82]
40 doz. 1611 - 5 oz. Tumbler - Ruby	44.00	[Fig. 104]
25 doz. 1611 High Footed Sherbet - Ruby	43.75	[Heacock, Fenton 2, p. 82]
20 doz. 1611 Cordial - Ruby	20.00	[Fig. 97]
10 doz. 1611 Low Sherbet - Ruby	11.00	[Heacock, Fenton 2, p. 82]
8 doz. 1611 Cups - Ruby	12.00	

Fenton Inventory, Ruby Glass Entries (*continued*)

Description of items	Inventory Value	Reference
15 doz. 1611 Saucers - Ruby	22.50	[Heacock, Fenton 2, p. 82]
30 doz. 1611 - 9 oz. Footed Tumblers - Ruby	52.50	[Heacock, Fenton 2, p. 82]
14 doz. 1611 Cocktails - Ruby	21.00	[Heacock, Fenton 2, p. 82]
18 doz. 1611 Jug - Ruby	162.00	[Fig. 102]
35 doz. 1611 Finger Bowls - Ruby	78.75	[Heacock, Fenton 2, p. 82]
65 doz. 1611 - 8" Plates - Ruby	162.50	[Fig. 107]
25 doz. 1611 - 10" Plates - Ruby	87.50	[Eddie Unger, "Comparison of Fenton vs. Duncan & Miller Georgian", National Duncan Glass Journal, April-June, 1987, p.17; Edie Unger, "'Georgian' Controversy", Glass Review, November, 1987, p.2]
20 doz. 1611 - 6" Plates - Ruby	45.00	[Heacock, Fenton 2, p. 82]
30 doz. 1611 Sugar - Ruby	67.50	[Fig. 103]
60 doz. 1611 Cream - Ruby	135.00	[Fig. 103]
2 doz. 1611 Candlesticks - Ruby	6.00	["Recent Discoveries", Butterfly Net, January 1982, p. 8]
35 doz. 1611 Goblet - Ruby	61.15	[Fig. 105]
8 doz. 1611 Grill Plate - Ruby	36.00	[Fig. 473?]
5 doz. 1935 Decanter - Ruby	37.50	[Heacock, Fenton 2, p. 139]
100 doz. 1933 Tumblers - Ruby	81.00	[Heacock, Fenton 1, p.113]
50 doz. 1643 Flower Blocks - Jade, Ruby	40.50	[Fig. 99?]
20 doz. 1643 Nymph - Ruby & Jade	16.20	[Fig. 99?]
261 doz. 1234 - 6" Nappy - Ruby, Jade & Asstd	417.60	[Heacock, Fenton 1, p. 113?]
38 doz. 1234 Candlesticks - Ruby & Jade	30.78	["Answers from Mr. Frank Fenton", Butterfly Net, June 1980, p. 9]

Fenton Inventory, Ruby Glass Entries (*continued*)

Description of items	Inventory Value	Reference
200 doz. 848 Candlesticks - Ruby & Jade	162.00	[Fig. 101]
160 doz. 848 Ash Tray - Ruby & Jade	129.60	[Fig. 98]
13 doz. 1681 Baskets - Jade & Ruby	93.60	[Heacock, Fenton 2, pp. 66, 87, 97]
6 doz. 950 Candlesticks - Ruby	18.00	[Heacock, Fenton 2, pp. 86, 91, 92]
26 doz. 857 Fld & Fan Vase - Ruby, Black & Jade	171.60	[Heacock, Fenton 1, pp. 88, 92, 93; Heacock, Fenton 2, pp. 66, 87, 92, 93, 97]
5 doz. 185 - 6" Vase - Ruby	22.50	[Heacock, Fenton 2, p. 87]
16 doz. 184 - 12" Vase - Jade & Ruby	120.00	[Heacock, Fenton 2, p. 81, 87, 92, 93]
15 doz. 184 - 10" Vase - Ruby	90.00	[Heacock, Fenton 2, p. 81, 87, 92, 93, 97]
7 doz. 519 - 21" Vase - Ruby	63.00	
6 doz. 1639 Hdld Nappy - Ruby	36.00	
[?] 0 doz. 1502 Ftd. Tumbler - Ruby	52.50	[Heacock, Fenton 1, pp. 110?, 111?]
50 doz. 107 Vases - Ruby	165.00	[Heacock, Fenton 2, p. 96]
4 doz. 600 Fld Bowl - Ruby	30.00	[Heacock, Fenton 2, p. 87]
10 doz. 846 Fld Bowl - Ruby	60.00	[Heacock, Fenton 2, p. 67, 68, 94]
2 doz. 184 - 8" Vase-Cut - Ruby & Jade	15.00	[Heacock, Fenton 2, p. 81]
96 doz. 308 Cig. Box - M. Green, Ruby, Jade & Asstd	288.00	
1935		
35 doz. 1234 Candleholders - Ruby	28.35	["Answers from Mr. Frank Fenton", Butterfly Net, June 1980, p.9]
35 doz. 1903 - 8" Shal Nap - Ruby	61.25	[Heacock, Fenton 2, p. 96]
19 doz. 1620 Goblet - Ruby	33.25	[Heacock, Fenton 2, p. 30]
11 doz. 1620 Sherbet - Ruby	19.25	[Fig. 89]
10 doz. 1620 - 9 oz. Hi Ball - Ruby	13.50	[Heacock, Fenton 2, p. 83?]

Fenton Inventory, Ruby Glass Entries (*continued*)

Description of items	Inventory Value	Reference
16 doz. 1620 - 5 oz. Tumbler - Ruby	18.40	[Weatherman, Colored Glassware 2, p. 105, lower (5 oz.?)]
50 doz. 1620 - 7 oz. Old Fash. Cocktails - Ruby	67.50	[Heacock, Fenton 2, p. 83]
4 doz. 1620 Ice Pails - Ruby	28.80	[Heacock, Fenton 2, p. 83]
6 doz. 1620 - 2-1/2 oz. Whiskey - Ruby	6.60	[Heacock, Fenton 2, p. 83]
9 doz. 1620 - 8 oz.. Pilsner - Ruby	15.75	[Heacock, Fenton 2, p. 83]
22 doz. 1620 Cocktail Shaker - Ruby	330.00	[Heacock, Fenton 2, p. 83]
4 doz. 1620 - 8" Plate - Ruby	12.00	[Wheaterman, Colored Glassware 2, p. 105, lower (8"?)]
9 doz. 1639 - 8" Plate - Ruby	22.50	[Heacock, Fenton 2, p. 65]
18 doz. 1611 Salts - Ruby	54.00	[Fig. 106]
3 doz. 1611 Cr. Vase - Ruby	5.25	[Eddie Unger, "Comparison of Fenton vs Duncan & Miller Georgian", National Duncan Glass Journal, April-June, 1987, p.16?]
82 doz. 1611 - 9 oz. Tumblers - Ruby	90.20	[Heacock, Fenton 2, p. 82]
20 doz. 1611 Nut Dish - Ruby	20.00	[Heacock, Fenton 2, p. 82]
15 doz. 1611 Cordial - Ruby	15.00	[Heacock, Fenton 2, p. 82]
17 doz. 1611 - 12 oz. Ice Teas - Ruby	25.50	[Heacock, Fenton 2, p. 82]
6 doz. 1611 - 8" Plates - Ruby	15.00	[Fig. 107]
8 doz. 1611 12" Grill Plates - Ruby	36.00	[Fig. 473?]
6 doz. 1611 - 6" Plates - Ruby	13.50	[Heacock, Fenton 2, p. 82]
21 doz. 1611 Saucers - Ruby	31.50	[Heacock, Fenton 2, p. 82]

Fenton Inventory, Ruby Glass Entries *(continued)*

Description of items	Inventory Value	Reference
6 doz. 1611 - 10" Plates - Ruby	21.00	[Eddie Unger, "Comparison of Fenton vs Duncan & Miller Georgian", National Duncan Glass Journal, April-June, 1987, p.17; Edie Unger, "'Georgian' Controversy", Glass Review, November, 1987, p.2]
18 doz. 1611 Finger Bowls - Ruby	40.50	[Heacock, Fenton 2, p. 82]
36 doz. 1611 Wines - Ruby	59.40	[Heacock, Fenton 2, p. 82, claret?]
24 doz. 1611 Cocktails - Ruby	36.00	[Heacock, Fenton 2, p. 82]
24 doz. 1611 Goblets - Ruby	42.00	[Fig. 105]
8 doz. 1611 - 9 oz. Ftd. Tumbler - Ruby	14.00	[Heacock, Fenton 2, p. 82]
12 doz. 1611 Low Cupd Sherbets - Ruby	13.20	[Fig. 97]
46 doz. 1611 Cups - Ruby	69.00	[Heacock, Fenton 2, p. 82]
12 doz. 1611 High Footed Sherbets - Ruby	21.00	[Fig. 104]
18 doz. 1933 Tumblers - Ruby	14.58	[Heacock, Fenton 1, p.113]
4 doz. 857 Cr. - Ruby	26.40	[Heacock, Fenton 1, p. 92; Heacock, Fenton 2, pp. 66, 92?]
4 doz. 857 Fan Vase - Ruby	26.40	[Heacock, Fenton 1, pp. 88, 92, 93; Heacock, Fenton 2, pp. 66, 92, 93, 97]
12 doz. 1681 Baskets - Ruby	86.40	[Heacock, Fenton 2, pp. 66, 87, 97]
73 doz. 1934 - Whiskey - Crystal, Amber, Ruby & Blue	73.00	[Heacock, Fenton 2, p. 83]
3 doz. 519 - 20" Vase - Ruby	27.00	
16 doz. 1502 - 9 oz. Ftd. Tumblers - Ruby	28.00	[Heacock, Fenton 1, pp. 110?, 111?]
14 doz. 1934 Decanter - Ruby	105.00	[Heacock, Fenton 2, p. 83]

Fenton Inventory, Ruby Glass Entries (*continued*)

1936

Description of items	Inventory Value	Reference
60 doz. 1611-9 oz. Tumblers - Ruby	66.00	[Heacock, Fenton 2, p. 82]
75 doz. 1611-5 oz. Tumblers - Ruby	82.50	[Heacock, Fenton 2, p. 82]
60 doz. 1611-2-1/2 Whiskey - Ruby	66.00	[Heacock, Fenton 2, p. 82]
40 doz. 1611 - Low Ftd. Sherbets - Ruby	44.00	[Fig. 97]
18 doz. 1611 Fld Sherbets - L. F. Ruby	19.80	
4 doz. 1611-12 oz. Ice Teas - Ruby	6.00	[Heacock, Fenton 2, p. 82]
20 doz. 1611-6" Plates - Ruby	45.00	[Heacock, Fenton 2, p. 82]
30 doz. 1611-8" Plates - Ruby	75.00	[Fig. 107]
40 doz. 1611 Hi Footed Sherbets - Ruby	70.00	[Fig. 104]
34 doz. 1611 Footed Tumblers - Ruby	59.50	[Heacock, Fenton 2, p. 82]
34 doz. 1611 Goblets - Ruby	59.50	[Fig. 102; Heacock, Fenton 2, p. 82]
20 doz. 1611 Cordials - Ruby	20.00	[Heacock, Fenton 2, p. 82]
25 doz. 1611 Nut Cups - Ruby	25.00	[Heacock, Fenton 2, p. 82]
9 doz. 1611 - 54 oz. Jugs - Ruby	81.00	[Fig. 102; Heacock, Fenton 2, p. 82]
40 doz. 1611 Cups - Ruby	60.00	[Heacock, Fenton 2, p. 82]
50 doz. 1611 Cocktails - Ruby	75.00	[Heacock, Fenton 2, p. 82]
44 doz. 1611 4-1/2 oz. Clarets - Ruby	72.00	[Heacock, Fenton 2, p. 82]
12 doz. 1611 Salt Shakers only - Ruby	27.00	[Fig. 106]
36 doz. 1611 Saucers - Ruby	54.00	[Heacock, Fenton 2, p. 82]
20 doz. 1611 Sugars - Ruby	45.00	[Fig. 103]
20 doz. 1611 Creams - Ruby	45.00	[Fig. 103]
49 doz. 1611 Bon Bons - Ruby	53.90	["More Georgian?", National Duncan Glass
16 doz. 1611 Finger Bowls - Ruby	26.00	[Heacock, Fenton 2, p. 82]

Fenton Inventory, Ruby Glass Entries (*continued*)

Description of items	Inventory Value	Reference
22 doz. 1611 - 10" Plates - Ruby	77.00	[Eddie Unger, "Comparison of Fenton vs Duncan & Miller Georgian", National Duncan Glass Journal, April-June, 1987, p.17; Edie Unger, "'Georgian' Controversy", Glass Review, November, 1987, p. 2]
5 doz. 184 - 12" Vases - Ruby	37.50	[Heacock, Fenton 2, pp. 81, 87, 92, 93]
2 doz. 1620 Goblets - Ruby	3.50	[Heacock, Fenton 2, p. 30]
10 doz. 1620 Sherbets - Ruby	17.50	[Fig. 89]
7 doz. 1620 Old Fash. Cocktails - Ruby	9.45	[Heacock, Fenton 2, p. 83]
30 doz. 1620 - 9 oz. Tumblers - Ruby	15.00	[Weatherman, Colored Glassware 2, p. 105, lower (9 oz.?)]
3 doz. 1620 - 12 oz. Ice Teas - Ruby	5.10	[Heacock, Fenton 2, p. 30 (12 oz.?)]
12 doz. 1620 - 6" Plates - Ruby	30.00	
9 doz. 1800 - 14" Plates - Ruby & Crystal	43.20	[Heacock, Fenton 2, p. 90?]
4 doz. 1800 Regular Bowls - Ruby	36.00	[Heacock, Fenton 2, p. 90?]
18 doz. 1800 - 8" Plates - Ruby	24.00	[Heacock, Fenton 2, p. 90]
40 doz. 1800 Whiskey Glasses - Ruby	36.00	[Heacock, Fenton 2, p. 139?]
24 doz. 1800 - 12 oz. Ice Teas - Ruby	36.00	
6 doz. 1935 Bottles - Ruby	45.00	[Heacock, Fenton 2, p. 139?]
10 doz. 950 Candle Holders - Ruby	36.00	[Heacock, Fenton 2, pp. 86, 91, 92]
110 doz. 848 - 9" Flard Nappy - Ruby	176.00	[Fig. 100]
50 doz. 848 Ash Trays - Ruby	40.50	[Heacock, Fenton 1, p. 113]
40 doz. 1234 Candle Holders - Ruby	32.40	["Answers from Mr. Frank Fenton", Butterfly Net, June 1980, p. 9]

Fenton Inventory, Ruby Glass Entries *(continued)*

Description of items		Inventory Value	Reference
10 doz. 349 Vases - Ruby		90.00	[Heacock, Fenton 2, p. 38]
30 doz. 202 Ash Trays - Ruby		22.50	[Frank M. Fenton, "Fenton Coasters", Butterfly Net, January 1984, p.6]
35 doz. 1934 Whiskey - Ruby		43.75	[Heacock, Fenton 2, p. 83]
20 doz. 1502 - 9 oz. Goblets - Ruby		35.00	[Heacock, Fenton 1, p. 111]
16 doz. 1901 Candle Holders - Ruby		16.00	[Fig. 110]
20 doz. 1093 - 9" Nappies - Ruby		35.00	[Fig. 109; Heacock, Fenton 1, p. 113; Heacock, Fenton 2, p. 96]
380 doz. #6 Shells -	50 doz. Milk	380.00	["New Finds", Butterfly Net, May 1984, p. 8 and color page; "Ref: Colored Page", Butterfly Net, March 1986, p. 4 and color page]
	30 doz. Crystal		
	100 doz. Ruby		
	55 doz. Blue		
	15 doz. Amber		
	60 doz. Black		
	45 doz. Light Green		
	25 doz. Rose		
250 doz. #7 Shells -	60 doz. Ruby	375.00	["New Finds", Butterfly Net, May 1984, p. 8, and Heacock, Fenton 2, p. 31]
	55 doz. Crystal		
	65 doz. Milk		
	15 doz. Blue		
	40 doz. Amber		
	15 doz. Black		
12 doz. 175-8" Leaf Plates - Ruby		24.00	[Fig. 85]

Fenton Inventory, Ruby Glass Entries (*continued*)

Description of items	Inventory Value	Reference
6 doz. 175-12" Leaf Plates - Ruby	12.00	[Heacock, Fenton 2, p. 102 (12"?)]
1937		
135 doz. 1611-2-1/2 oz. Whiskey - Ruby	162.00	[Heacock, Fenton 2, p. 82]
115 doz. 1611 - 5 oz. Tumbler - Ruby	138.00	[Heacock, Fenton 2, p. 82]
60 doz. 1611 - 9 oz. Tumbler - Ruby	72.00	[Heacock, Fenton 2, p. 82]
20 doz. 1611 - Goblet - Ruby	40.00	[Fig. 105]
15 doz. 1611 Ftd. Tumbler - Ruby	30.00	[Heacock, Fenton 2, p. 82]
2 doz. 1611 Hi Ftd. Sherbet - Ruby	4.00	[Fig. 104]
35 doz. 1611 Low Ftd. Sherbet - Ruby	43.75	[Fig. 97]
1 doz. 1611 Jug - Ruby	9.00	[Fig. 102; Heacock, Fenton 2, p. 82]
25 doz. 1611 - 6" Plate - Ruby	62.50	[Heacock, Fenton 2, p. 82]
30 doz. 1611 - 8" Plate - Ruby	90.00	[Fig. 107]
2 doz. 1611 - 10" Plate - Ruby	7.50	[Eddie Unger, "Comparison of Fenton vs Duncan & Miller Georgian", National Duncan Glass Journal, April-June, 1987, p. 17; Edie Unger, "'Georgian' Controversy", Glass Review, November, 1987, p. 2
10 doz. 1611 - 12" Grill Plate - Ruby	60.00	[Fig. 473?]
10 doz. 1611 Salt & Peppers - Ruby	60.00	[Fig. 106]
13 doz. 1611 4-1/2 oz. Claret - Ruby	23.40	[Heacock, Fenton 2, p. 82]
15 doz. 1611 Sugar & Creamers - Ruby	67.50	[Fig. 103]
10 doz. 1611 Cups - Ruby	17.50	[Heacock, Fenton 2, p. 82]
18 doz. 1611 Saucer - Ruby	21.00	[Heacock, Fenton 2, p. 82]
30 doz. 1800 - 6" Vase - Ruby	52.50	[Figs. 113-115; Heacock, Fenton 2, p. 90]
14 doz. 1800 Candlestick - Ruby	63.00	[Heacock, Fenton 2, p. 90]

Fenton Inventory, Ruby Glass Entries (*continued*)

Description of items	Inventory Value	Reference
25 doz. 1800 - 10" Bowl - Ruby	225.00	[Heacock, Fenton 2, p. 90 (10"?)]
18 doz. 1800 - 8" Plate - Ruby	54.00	[Heacock, Fenton 2, p. 90]
9 doz. 1800 Plate - Ruby	40.50	
36 doz. 1800 Whiskey - Ruby	28.80	[Heacock, Fenton 2, p. 139?]
30 doz. 1800 - 5 oz. Tumbler - Ruby	28.50	
6 doz. 1800 - 9 oz. Tumbler - Ruby	6.60	[Heacock, Fenton 2, pp. 35?, 36?; William Heacock, "Is It Fenton - or Is It Memorex?", Glass Collector, Summer, 1982, p. 19]
90 doz. 848 Bowl - Jade & Ruby	162.00	[Fig. 100; Heacock, Fenton 1, p. 91; Heacock, Fenton 2, p. 64]
85 doz. 1235-5" Nappy - Ruby	127.50	
75 doz. 639-6" Nappy - Ruby	131.25	
215 doz. 681-8" Plate - Ruby	376.25	[Frank M. Fenton, "Fenton Coasters", Butterfly Net, January 1984, p. 6]
95 doz. 680-6" Plate - Ruby	152.00	[Frank M. Fenton, "Fenton Coasters", Butterfly Net, January 1984, p. 6; Heacock, Fenton 2, pp. 112, 116, 117]
45 doz. 7 Sugar - Ruby	85.50	
53 doz. 7 Creamer - Ruby	100.70	
85 doz. 31 Cups - Ruby	97.75	
36 doz. 31 Saucer - Ruby	41.40	
36 doz. 1623 Candlestick - Ruby	41.40	[Fig. 90; Heacock, Fenton 1, pp. 92, 93, 111]
28 doz. 2000-11" Nappy - Ruby	112.00	[Heacock, Fenton 2, pp. 31?, 91?]
60 doz. 1502 Salt & Peppers - Ruby	138.00	["This and That The Elusive 'Diamond Optic'", Butterfly Net, July 1981, p. 8?]

Fenton Inventory, Ruby Glass Entries (*continued*)

Description of items	Inventory Value	Reference
18 doz. 835 Cr. Comport - Ruby	27.00	[Heacock, Fenton 2, p. 66]
8 doz. 1620-6" Plates - Ruby	18.00	
2 doz. 1620-8" Plates - Ruby	6.60	[Weatherman, Colored Glassware 2, p. 105, lower (8"?)]
10 doz. 1620-5 oz. Tumblers - Ruby	12.50	[Weatherman, Colored Glassware 2, p. 105, lower (5 oz.?)]
15 doz. 1620-9 oz. Tumblers - Ruby	16.50	[Weatherman, Colored Glassware 2, p. 105, lower (9 oz.?)]
12 doz. 1620-9 oz. Hi Balls - Ruby	18.00	[Heacock, Fenton 2, p. 83?]
10 doz. 1620-12 oz. Ice Tea - Ruby	15.00	[Heacock, Fenton 2, p. 30 (12 oz.?)]
25 doz. 1620 Wine - Ruby	45.00	[Heacock, Fenton 2, p. 83]
2 doz. 1620 Goblet - Ruby	3.76	[Weatherman, Colored Glassware 2, p. 105, lower]
2 doz. 1620 Cocktail Shaker - Ruby	30.00	[Heacock, Fenton 2, p. 83]
35 doz. 1502-9 oz. Bridge Goblet - Ruby	61.25	[Heacock, Fenton 1, p. 111]
24 doz. 1720-8" Plates - Ruby	54.00	
30 doz. 1720 Wines - Ruby	60.00	[Heacock, Collecting Glass, Vol. 1, p. 69 and back cover]
25 doz. 1720 Goblet - Ruby	50.00	[Heacock, Collecting Glass, Vol. 2, pp. 43, 45]
30 doz. 1720 Ice Tea - Ruby	67.50	
15 doz. 1720 Sherbet - Ruby	30.00	
4 doz. 1561 Lamp - Ruby & Roy Blue	36.00	
4 doz. 1563 Lamp - Ruby & Roy Blue	36.00	
45 doz. 1900/1 Hat - Ruby	90.00	[Heacock, Fenton 2, p. 60, Fig. 503]
50 doz. 1900/2 Hat - Ruby	150.00	[Heacock, Fenton 2, p. 89]
1-1/2 doz. 1900/3 Hat - Ruby	9.00	[Heacock, Fenton 2, p. 57, Fig. 450]

Fenton Inventory, Ruby Glass Entries *(continued)*

Description of items	Inventory Value	Reference
32 doz. 957 Fan - Ruby	1440.00	[Heacock, Fenton 2, p. 89]
40 doz. 1900 Ash Tray - Ruby	50.00	[Heacock, Fenton 2, p. 89]
75 doz. 1900 Slipper - Ruby	225.00	[Heacock, Fenton 2, p. 89]
5 doz. 1900-10" Bowls - Ruby	36.00	[Heacock, Fenton 2, p. 81]
4 doz. 1900 Fan Vase - Ruby	28.80	[Heacock, Fenton 2, p. 89]
1938		
45 doz. 957 Fan Trays - Ruby	202.50	[Heacock, Fenton 2, p. 89]
35 doz. 1611 Ice Teas - Ruby	48.30	[Heacock, Fenton 2, p. 82]
60 doz. 1611-9 oz. Tumblers - Ruby	72.00	[Heacock, Fenton 2, p. 82]
78 doz. 1611-5 oz. Tumblers - Ruby	93.60	[Heacock, Fenton 2, p. 82]
10 doz. 1611 High Footed Sherbets - Ruby	20.00	[Fig. 104]
20 doz. 1611 Salt & Peppers - Ruby	120.00	Fig. 106]
40 doz. 1611 Sherbets - Ruby	50.00	[Fig. 97]
38 doz. 1611 Goblets - Ruby	76.00	[Fig. 105]
8 doz. 1611 Clarets - Ruby	14.40	[Heacock, Fenton 2, p. 82]
24 doz. 1611 Cocktail - Ruby	42.00	[Heacock, Fenton 2, p. 82]
30 doz. 1611 Sugar & Cream sets - Ruby	135.00	[Fig. 103]
9 doz. 1611 Grill Plates - Ruby	54.00	[Fig. 473]
18 doz. 1611-10" Plates - Ruby	67.50	[Eddie Unger, "Comparison of Fenton vs Duncan & Miller Georgian", National Duncan Glass Journal, April-June, 1987, p. 17; Eddie Unger, "'Georgian' Controversy", Glass Review, November, 1987, p. 2]
30 doz. 1611-8" Plates - Ruby	90.00	[Fig. 107]
60 doz. 1611-6" Plates - Ruby	150.00	[Heacock, Fenton 2, p. 82]

Fenton Inventory, Ruby Glass Entries (*continued*)

Description of items	Inventory Value	Reference
15 doz. 1611 Cups & Saucers - Ruby	52.50	[Heacock, Fenton 2, p. 82]
15 doz. 1611 Jugs - Ruby	135.00	[Fig. 102; Heacock, Fenton 2, p. 82]
20 doz. 1620 Goblets - Ruby	38.60	[Weatherman, Colored Glassware 2, p. 105, lower]
20 doz. 1620 Sherbets - Ruby	38.60	[Fig. 89]
20 doz. 1620 Cocktail - Ruby	36.00	[Heacock, Fenton 2, pp. 83 (wine)?, 138?]
7 doz. 1620 Ice Teas - Ruby	13.16	[Heacock, Fenton 2, p. 30?]
12 doz. 1620-9 oz. High Balls - Ruby	18.00	[Heacock, Fenton 2, p. 83 (9 oz.?)]
18 doz. 1620-9 oz. Tumblers - Ruby	24.84	[Weatherman, Colored Glassware 2, p. 105, lower (9 oz.?)]
14 doz. 1620-5 oz. Tumblers - Ruby	17.50	[Weatherman, Colored Glassware 2, p. 105, lower (5 oz.?)]
8 doz. 1620-6" Plates - Ruby	22.00	
15 doz. 1620-10 oz. Pilsners - Ruby	28.95	[Heacock, Fenton 2, p. 83 (10 oz.?)]
15 doz. 848-6" Nappies - Ruby	27.00	[Fig. 100?; Heacock, Fenton 1, p. 91 (6"?); Heacock, Fenton 2, p. 64 (6"?)]
100 doz. 1700 Ash Trays - Ruby	75.00	
45 doz. #7 Sugar & Cream Sets - Ruby	126.00	
80 doz. #31 Cups - Ruby	92.00	
54 doz. #31 Saucers - Ruby	62.10	
42 #680 Plates - Ruby	67.20	[Frank M. Fenton, "Fenton Coasters", Butterfly Net, January 1984, p. 6; Heacock, Fenton 2, pp. 112, 116, 117]
3 doz. 682 Plates - Ruby	10.80	[Frank M. Fenton, "Fenton Coasters", Butterfly Net, January 1984, p. 6?; Heacock, Fenton 2, p. 102?

Fenton Inventory, Ruby Glass Entries (*continued*)

Description of items	Inventory Value	Reference
11 doz. 2000-7" Nappy - Ruby	44.00	[Heacock, Fenton 2, p. 95?]
12 doz. 1720 Goblets - Ruby	27.00	[Heacock, Collecting Glass, Vol. 2, pp. 43,45]
14 doz. 1720 Cocktail - Ruby	31.50	
10 doz. 1720 Bon Bon - Asstd Shapes - Ruby	22.50	Lechler, Book 1, p. 41 bottom left (bon bon?)
18 doz. 1720 Ice Teas - Ruby	40.50	
10 doz. 1900-2 Baskets - Ruby	37.50	[Heacock, Fenton 2, p. 60, Fig. 503]
15 doz. 1900/3 Baskets - Ruby	108.00	[Heacock, Fenton 2, pp. 60 (Fig. 493)?, 76 (#1936)?, 130 (#1936)?]
50 doz. 1900/1 Hats - Ruby	100.00	[Heacock, Fenton 2, p. 60, Fig. 503]
50 doz. 1900 Slippers - Ruby	150.00	[Heacock, Fenton 2, p. 89]
8 doz. 1900 Bootees - Ruby	16.00	[Heacock, Fenton 2, pp. 76 (#1994)?, 130 (#1994)?]
40 doz. 1900/2 Hats - Ruby	120.00	[Heacock, Fenton 2, p. 89]
10 doz. 1900/3 Hats - Ruby	60.00	[Heacock, Fenton 2, p. 57, Fig. 450]
10 doz. 1900 Ash Trays - Ruby 1939	12.50	[Heacock, Fenton 2, p. 89]
2 doz. 1900-2 Med. Hats - Ruby	6.00	Heacock, Fenton 2, p. 89]
36 doz. 1900-1 Small Hat - Ruby	72.00	[Heacock, Fenton 2, p. 60, Fig. 503]
1-1/2 doz. 1611 Goblet - Ruby	3.00	[Fig. 105]
7 doz. 1611 Ftd. Tumbler - Ruby	14.00	[Heacock, Fenton 2, p. 82]
8 doz. 1611 Hi Ftd. Sherbet - Ruby	16.00	[Fig. 104]
22 doz. 1611 Cupd Sherbet - Ruby	27.50	[Fig. 97]
6 doz. 1611 5" Grill Plates - Ruby	16.00	
40 doz. 1611 6" Grill Plates - Ruby	100.00	
12 doz. 1611 Saucer - Ruby	21.00	[Heacock, Fenton 2, p. 82]

Fenton Inventory, Ruby Glass Entries (*continued*)

Description of items	Inventory Value	Reference
24 doz. 1611 Cups - Ruby	42.00	[Heacock, Fenton 2, p. 82]
7/12 doz. 1611 Jugs - Ruby	5.25	[Fig. 102; Heacock, Fenton 2, p. 82]
2 doz. 1611 12 oz. Ice Teas - Ruby	3.20	[Heacock, Fenton 2, p. 82]
2 doz. 1611 Salt - Ruby	6.00	[Fig. 106]
2 doz. 1611 Finger Bowls - Ruby	5.00	[Heacock, Fenton 2, p. 82]
18 doz. 1611 Sugars - Ruby	45.50?	[Fig. 103]
4 doz. 1611 Cream - Ruby	6.00	[Fig. 103]
40 doz. 1611 Bon-Bons - Asst. Shapes - Ruby	50.00	["More Georgian?", National Duncan Glass Journal, July-September, 1987, fourth page of article?]
14 doz. 1611 Whiskey - Ruby	16.80	[Heacock, Fenton 2, p. 82]
3/4 doz. 1620 Goblet - Ruby	1.44	[Weatherman, Colored Glassware 2, p. 105, lower]
1/3 doz. 1620 Sherbet - Ruby	.64	[Fig. 89]
1-1/2 doz. 1620 12 oz. Ice Tea - Ruby	2.82	[Heacock, Fenton 2, p. 30 (12 oz.?)]
20 doz. 1620 9 oz. Tumbler - Ruby	27.40	[Weatherman, Colored Glassware 2, p. 105, lower (9 oz.?)]
8 doz. 1620 9 oz. Hi Ball - Ruby	12.00	[Heacock, Fenton 2, p. 83 (9 oz.?)]
3 doz. 1620 5 oz. Tumbler - Ruby	3.75	[Weatherman, Colored Glassware 2, p. 105, lower (5 oz.?)]
1 doz. 1620 8" Plate - Ruby	3.30	[Weatherman, Colored Glassware 2, p. 105, lower, (8"?)]
20 doz. 1620 6" Plate - Ruby	55.00	
2/3 doz. 1620 Cocktail - Ruby	1.20	[Heacock, Fenton 2, pp. 83 (wine)?, 138?]
30 doz. 1800 Ice Tea - Ruby	45.00	

Fenton Inventory, Ruby Glass Entries *(continued)*

Description of items	Inventory Value	Reference
1941		
240 doz. 1611-9 oz. Tumbler - Ruby 3 oz.	372.00	[Heacock, Fenton 2, p. 82]
12 doz. 1611-12 oz. Ice Tea - Ruby	27.00	[Heacock, Fenton 2, p. 82]
180 doz. 1611 Goblets - Ruby	495.00	[Fig. 105]
25 doz. 1611 H.F. Sherbets - Ruby	68.75	[Fig. 104]
18 doz. 1611 Ftd. Tumblers - Ruby	49.50	[Heacock, Fenton 2, p. 82]
20 doz. 1611-8" Plates - Ruby	66.00	[Fig. 107]
50 doz. 1611 T.F. Sherbet - Ruby	87.50	[Fig. 97?]
20 doz. 1611- 5 oz. Tumbler - Ruby	31.00	[Heacock, Fenton 2, p. 82]
1942		
14 doz. 1611 Goblets - Ruby	38.50	[Fig. 105]
36 doz. 1611 Tumblers - Ruby	55.80	[Heacock, Fenton 2, p. 82]

End of Fenton Inventory, Ruby Glass Entries

CROWN COLLECTION

WINDSOR CROWN

		Retail Price Ea.
2749/133	Bottle & Stopper..........Crystal	$275
	Gold or Royal Blue	3.50
	Height 4¾ in.	
2749/314	3½ in. Candleholder .... Crystal	2.00
	Gold or Royal Blue	2.50
2749/386	Footed Chalice & Cover	
	Crystal	7.00
	Gold or Royal Blue	7.50
	Ruby	8.50
	Height 8½ in.	
2749/388	Footed Chalice.............Crystal	4.75
	Gold or Royal Blue	5.25
	Ruby	6.00
	Height 6¾ in.	
2749/676	Candy & Cover.............Crystal	5.50
	Gold or Royal Blue	6.00
	Ruby	6.75
	Height 5½ in.	
2749/677	Candy ....Crystal	3.25
	Gold or Royal Blue	3.75
	Ruby	4.25
	Height 3¾ in.	

HAPSBURG CROWN

2750/386	Footed Chalice & Cover	
	Crystal	$7.00
	Gold or Royal Blue	7.50
	Ruby	8.50
	Height 9¼ in.	
2750/388	Footed Chalice.............Crystal	4.75
	Gold or Royal Blue	5.25
	Ruby	6.00
	Height 7¼ in.	
2750/676	Candy & Cover.............Crystal	5.50
	Gold or Royal Blue	6.00
	Ruby	6.75
	Height 5¾ in.	
2750/677	Candy ....Crystal	3.25
	Gold or Royal Blue	3.75
	Ruby	4.25
	Height 3¾ in.	

NAVARRE CROWN

2751/195	9	in. Bowl ....Crystal	$5.50
		Gold or Royal Blue	6.25
		Ruby	7.00
		Height 4½ in.	
2751/198	9	in. Bowl & Cover.............Crystal	9.00
		Gold or Royal Blue	10.00
		Ruby	11.25
		Height 8⅛ in.	
2751/199	9	in. Footed Bowl.............Crystal	8.50
		Gold or Royal Blue	8.75
		Ruby	10.50
		Height 8¼ in.	
2751/203	9	in. Footed Bowl & Cover..Crystal	12.00
		Gold or Royal Blue	12.50
		Ruby	14.75
		Height 12⅛ in.	

LUXEMBOURG CROWN

2766/311	Trindle Candle Bowl.....Crystal	$7.00
	Gold or Royal Blue	7.50
	Ruby	8.00
	Height 4¾ in. - Diam. 7¼ in.	

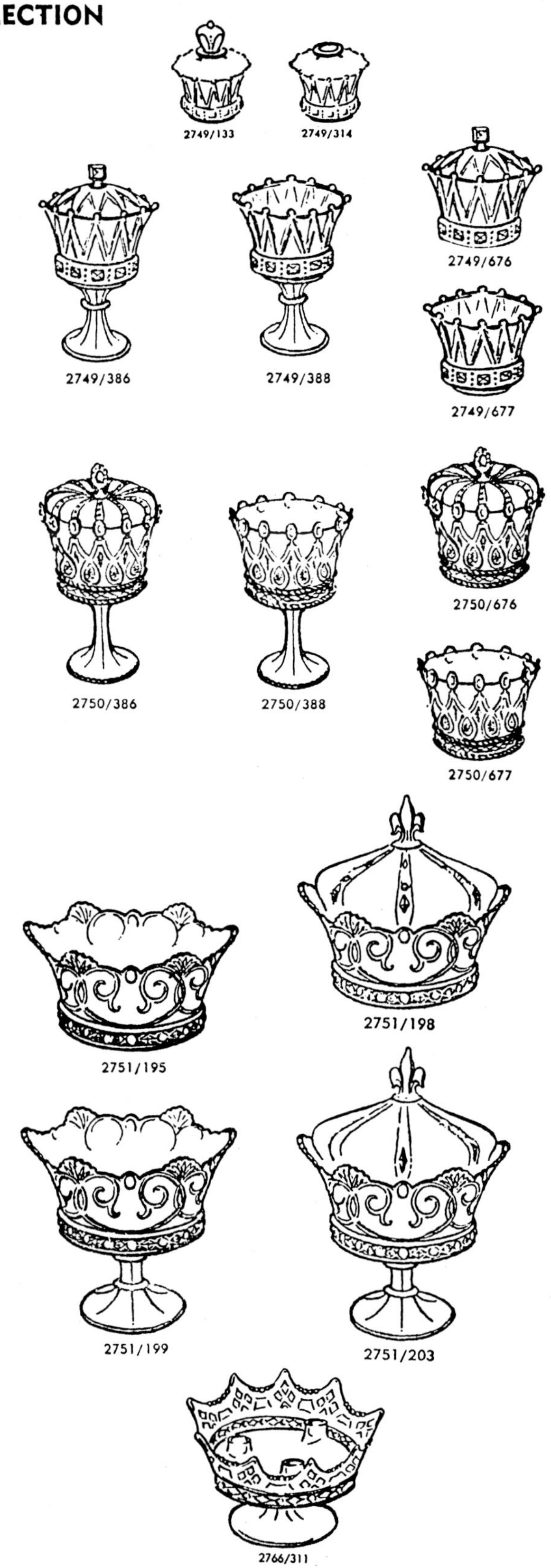

2749/133   2749/314

2749/676

2749/386   2749/388

2749/677

2750/386   2750/388

2750/676

2750/677

2751/195

2751/198

2751/199

2751/203

2766/311

Fostoria catalogue page (note date).

DUNCAN'S RUBY STEMWARE
Made in Ruby Bowl with Crystal Stem and Foot

	GRANADA No. 504 Pattern *List Dozen*	DIAMOND No. 5375 Pattern *List Dozen*	DOVER No. 5330 Pattern *List Dozen*
Goblet	$30.00	$24.00	$24.00
Saucer Champagne or Tall Sherbet	30.00	24.00	24.00
Liquor Cocktail	30.00	24.00	24.00
Wine	30.00	24.00	24.00
Cordial	30.00	24.00	24.00
Seafood Cocktail	30.00	24.00	24.00
Footed Ice Tea	30.00	24.00	24.00
Footed Juice	30.00	24.00	24.00
Finger Bowl	30.00	24.00	24.00
No. 30— 6 in. Plate	14.40	14.40	14.40
No. 30— 7½ in. Plate	16.50	16.50	16.50
No. 30— 8½ in. Plate	21.00	21.00	21.00
No. 30—10½ in. Plate	30.00	30.00	30.00

DUNCAN'S RUBY DECORATIVE PIECES TO HARMONIZE WITH RUBY STEMWARE

		List Doz.
30	Small Duck Ash Tray	$ 15.00
71-D	Candlestick	18.00
72-G	Bowl	60.00
72-E	8 in. Vase	60.00
76-A	14 in. Plate	60.00
113	14 in. Plate	45.00
115	9 in. Crimped Bowl	36.00
115	10 in. Oval Bowl	36.00
115	10½ in. Crimped Bowl	48.00
115	11½ in. Oval Bowl	48.00
115	6 in. High Foot Comport, Ruby Bowl and Stem, Crystal Foot	42.00
115	8 in. 3 Hld. 3 Cpt. Candy Box & Cover	48.00
115	5½ in. Footed Candy Jar and Cover	60.00
115	11 in. 2 Handled Sandwich Tray	42.00
115	8 in. 3 Hld. 3 Compt. Relish Tray	30.00
115	4½ in. Club Ash Tray	21.00
115	5½ in. Flower Arranger	36.00
115	8½ in. Flower Arranger	54.00
121	Cornucopia, No. 2 Shape	60.00

		List Doz.
506	9 in. Bud Vase, Ruby Bowl, Crys. Ft.	$ 24.00
528	5½ in. Ring Hld. Urn, Sq. Ft. Ruby Bowl, Crystal Hdls. and Foot	39.00
527	5½ in. Vase, Square Foot, Ruby Bowl, Crystal Foot	30.00
529	7 in. Urn, Ruby, Crystal Foot	36.00
538	3½ in. Cigarette Holder, Ruby Bowl Crystal Foot	24.00
539	3½ in. Handled Cigarette Holder, Ruby Bowl, Crystal Hdls. and Foot	30.00
538	3 pc. Cigarette Set, Ruby	30.00
539	3 pc. Handled Cigarette Set, Ruby	36.00
555	6 in. Square Foot Comport, Ruby Bowl, Crystal Stem and Foot	60.00
30½	3½ in. Swan, Ruby Bowl, Crystal Neck	15.00
30½	6 in. Swan, Ruby Bowl, Crystal Neck	21.00
30½	7 in. Swan, Ruby Bowl, Crystal Neck	21.00
30½	10½ in. Swan, Ruby Bowl, Crystal Neck	42.00
30½	12 in. Swan, Ruby Bowl, Crystal Neck	54.00

PUNCH BOWL SETS
Made in Crystal

		List Dozen
113½	15 pc. Punch Set, All Crystal	$216.00
	Consisting of: 1/12 doz. 1½ gallon Punch Bowl 1 doz. Punch Cups 1/12 doz. 18 in. Punch Bowl Tray, Roll. Edge 1/12 doz. Punch Ladle	
118½	15 pc. Punch Set, All Crystal	$180.00
	Consisting of: 1/12 doz. 1 gallon Punch Bowl 1 doz. Punch Cups 1/12 doz. 16 in. Punch Bowl Tray, Roll. Edge 1/12 doz. Punch Ladle	

		List Dozen
126	14 pc. Punch Set, All Crystal	$198.00
	Consisting of: 1/12 doz. Punch Bowl 1 doz. Punch Cups 1/12 doz. Punch Ladle	
126	14 pc. Punch Set, Crystal w/Ruby Hdls.	$216.00
	Consisting of: 1/12 doz. Punch Bowl 1 doz. Punch Cups, Ruby Handled 1/12 doz. Punch Ladle, Ruby Handled	

PUNCH BOWLS, CUPS, LADLES and TRAYS
Made in Crystal

		List Dozen
113	1½ gallon Punch Bowl	$ 54.00
118	1 gallon Punch Bowl	45.00
126	Punch Bowl	72.00
113½	5 oz. Punch Cup	6.00
118½	5 oz. Punch Cup	6.00
126	Punch Cup, All Crystal	9.00
126	Punch Cup, Crystal W/Ruby Handles	10.80

		List Dozen
113	Punch Ladle	$ 18.00
118	Punch Ladle	18.00
126	Punch Ladle, All Crystal	18.00
126	Punch Ladle, Crystal W/Ruby Handles	21.00
113	18 in. Punch Bowl Tray, Rolled Edge	78.00
118	16 in. Punch Bowl Tray, Rolled Edge	45.00

From Duncan and Miller Glass Company Price List, January 1, 1951, pages 10 and 12.

PLAIN . . . OR IN COMBINATION WITH GREEN OR ROYAL RUBY

Most milk glass has been in traditional shapes. Here you find it in smart new modern pieces that will open up a whole new market for orders. Ask your Duncan salesman for complete list of items . . . or write direct to us.

THE DUNCAN & MILLER GLASS CO.
WASHINGTON, PA.

The Loveliest Glassware in America

Announcing
A DARING NEW APPROACH TO AN OLD MATERIAL

Milk Glass
that is MODERN . . . NEW

Duncan and Miller advertisement. See Figure 63.

These Birds Pay Off

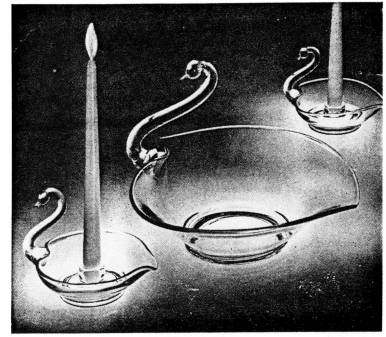

3-Piece Swan-Neck Console Set
11½" Bowl, Two 5" Candlesticks
No. 992—1S

5" Swan-Neck Dish
No. 974—1S

5" Heart-Shaped
Bon Bon Dish
No. 978

6" Basket
No. 975

Push The Popular Viking Line

Favorite hand made quality crystal

... featured in national magazines ... countrywide

sure-sellers ... Stock and show the whole line in its seven attractive

colors: all-crystal, evergreen, ruby, sky-blue, amber,

cobalt, and ebony ... Order by number from Viking today.

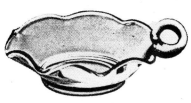

6" Bon Bon Dish
No. 979

VIKING HAND MADE *Treasured American Glass*

MADE ONLY BY VIKING GLASS COMPANY • NEW MARTINSVILLE, WEST VIRGINIA

Viking Glass Company advertisement. See Figure 64.

FANCY GLASSWARE

"IMPERIAL"—Hand made, quality glassware, full finished, brilliantly fire polished. Lovely colored, white and crystal glassware in popular patterns! Illustrations are ACTUAL PHOTOGRAPHS.

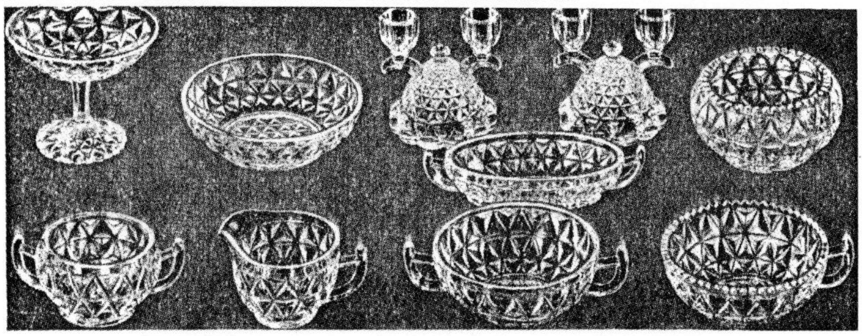

"MT. VERNON"—CRYSTAL—PRISM DESIGN

11 KINDS OF PIECES—Early American pattern with allover heavy pressed prism design.

¼ Doz Each Of The Following:

Square Nappy, 7 in.	Creamer, 3½ in. high
Round Nappy, 7 in.	Sugar Bowl, 3 in. high
Ice Tub, 5½ in.	Handled Olive Dish, 5¾ in.
Rose Bowl, 6 in.	Handled Celery Dish, 6½ in.
Comport, 4¾ in.	Handled Bonbon, 5¾ in.

And ½ doz Double Socket Candlesticks, 4½ in.

50R-4502—
3 doz in carton, 38 lbs
DOZ $1.44

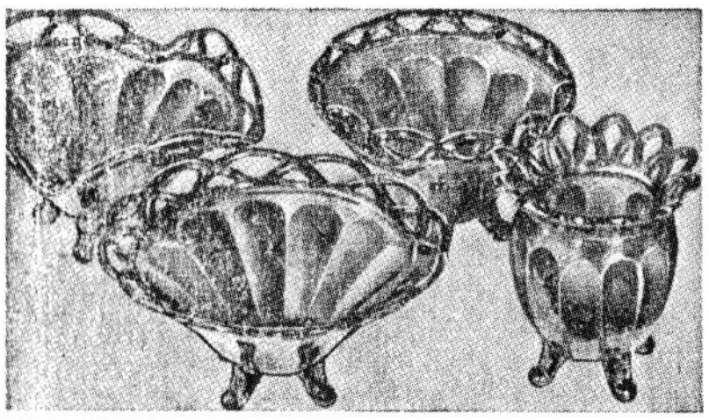

CRYSTAL & COLORED—LACE EDGE

4 KINDS OF PIECES—Optic design, with openwork lace edge, FOOTED, asst. 12 crystal, 4 dark blue, 4 forest green and 4 amber.

½ Doz Each Of The Following:
Flared Bowl, 7½ in.
Rose Bowl, 6½ in.
Flower Vase, 5 in. high
Square Bowl, 6¾ in.

$1.80 DOZ

50R-4520—2 doz in carton, 33 lbs

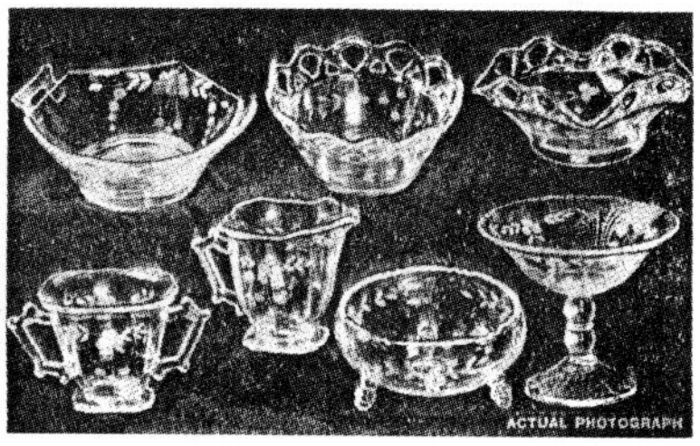

GENUINE CUT CRYSTAL

8 KINDS OF PIECES—Cut floral & leaf design.

¼ Doz Each Of Following:
3-Footed Lily Bowl, 5½ in.
3-Footed Nut Bowl, 6½ in.
Footed Comport, 4½ in. high
Cream Pitcher, 3½ in. high
Sugar Bowl, 3½ in. high
Lace Edge Square Bonbon, 5¼ in.
Lace Edge Nut Bowl, 5¾ in.
Lace Edge Shallow Bonbon, 6½ in.

$1.80 DOZ

50R-4521—2 doz in carton, 22 lbs

It's Easy to Buy from BUTLER BROTHERS

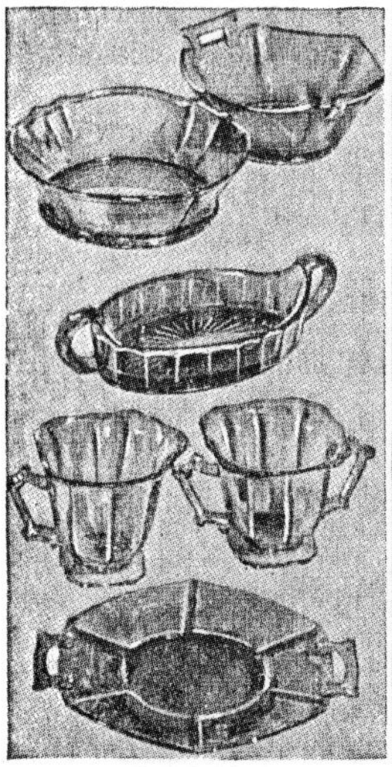

RICH RUBY COLOR

6 KINDS OF PIECES — High quality ruby red glass, attractive panel design.

⅓ Doz Each Of Following:
2-Handled Bonbon, 6½ in.
2-Handled Plate, 8 in.
2 Handled Oval Pickle Dish, 8½ in.
Round Nappy, 6½ in.
Handled Creamer, 3½ in. high
Sugar Bowl, 3½ in. high

50R-4523—
2 doz in ctn, 25 lbs
$1.95 DOZ

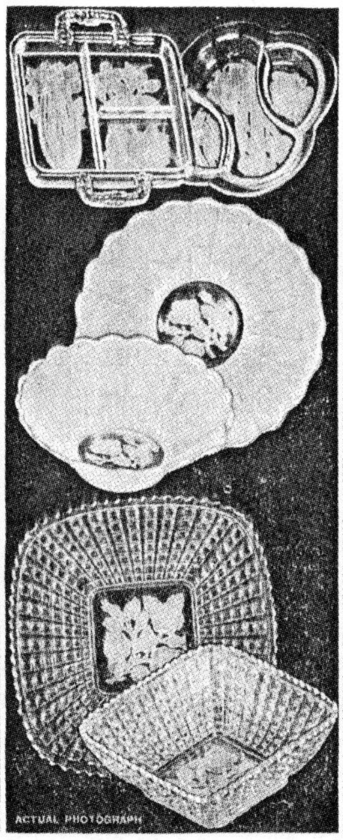

INTAGLIO ETCHED

6 KINDS OF PIECES — Beautiful crystal glass with deeply impressed intaglio bottom designs.

⅙ Doz Each of Following:
Handled Relish Dish, 9¾ x 7¼ in.
Oval Relish Dish, 9¼ x 8½ in.
Cake Plate, 7½ in., white frosted
Round Bowl, 8¾ in., white frosted
Square Plate, 11 in., jewel pattern
Square Bowl, 7¾ in., jewel pattern

50R-4543—
1 doz in ctn, 30 lbs
$3.75 DOZ

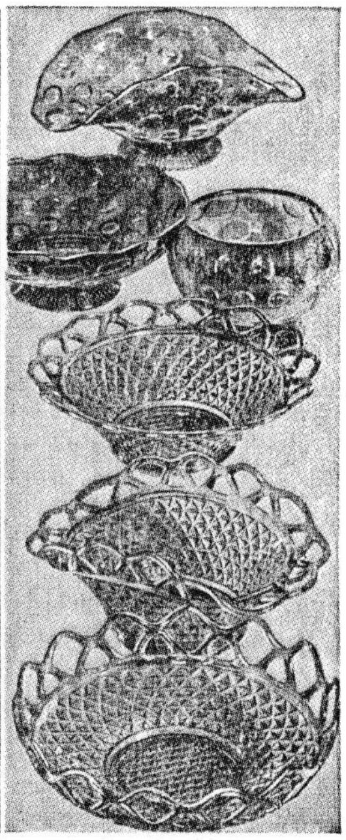

RICH RUBY GLASS

6 KINDS OF PIECES—High grade quality, rich ruby red glass, popular prism and bulls-eye patterns.

⅙ Doz Each Of Following:
Footed Bowl, 9 in.
Footed Rose Bowl, 6¼ in.
Footed Basket, 10 in. high
Lace Edge Shallow Bowl, 9½ in.
Lace Edge Flared Bowl, 9½ in.
Lace Edge Basket, 9½ in. high

50R-4541—
1 doz in ctn, 28 lbs
$3.85 DOZ

Ruby and other glass made by Imperial Glass Corporation, as shown in a Butler Brothers Winter and Holiday 1939 catalogue. The pattern which Butler Brothers called Cristolbrite has never before been identified as Imperial, to this writer's knowledge.

NOW AT A LOW PRICE!

MATCHING

RUBY GLASS

A Window Leader To Sell Separately and as a 7-Pc. Set—1 Bowl and 6 Nappies. Mitre and panel designs, double handled.

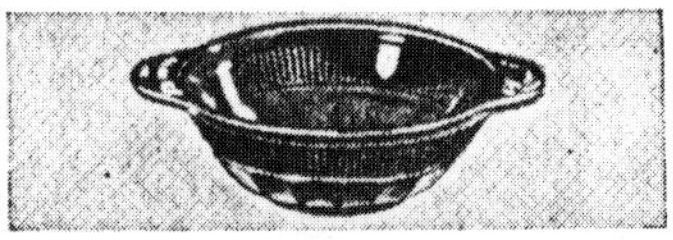

4½ IN. NAPPY

50R-3913—6 doz in carton, 23 lbs.

Doz **27c**

Regular Price After August 31 Will Be 30c Doz

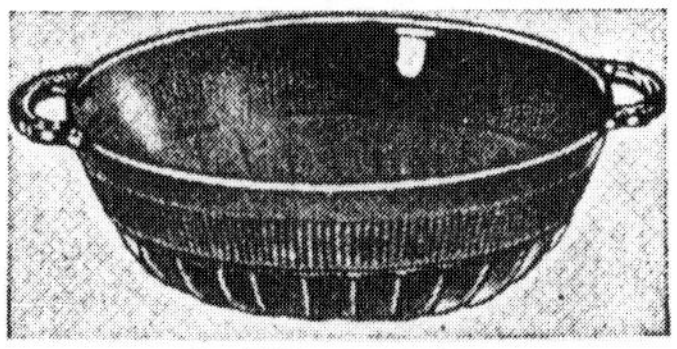

8 IN. BOWL

50R-3933—1 doz in carton, 16 lbs.

Doz **79c**

Regular Price After August 31 Will Be 85c Doz

From Butler Brothers' Fall 1940 catalogue. See Figures 170, 170A and 174.

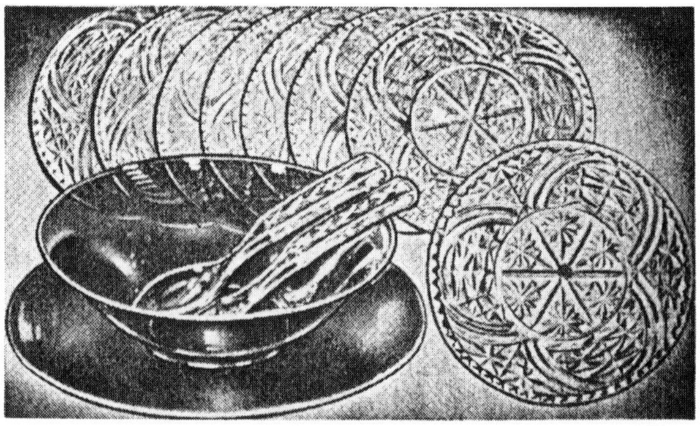

Combine Ruby and Crystal for Sales

Buy the 4-pc. royal ruby glass salad set with prescut crystal fork and spoon or a set of 12 pieces to sell at prices absurdly low. Here is a fine opportunity for big promotion.

4 Pc. Set $6.75 Doz Sets

4-Pc. Ruby Glass Set
11½ in. royal ruby glass bowl
13¼ in. royal ruby glass tray
9¾ in. Crystal Spoon and Fork
Pieces packed separately for safety.
50R-3995—1 doz sets in 3 ctns., 70 lbs..........Doz sets 6.75

12-Pc. Combination Sets
11½ in. royal ruby salad bowl
13¼ in. ruby serving bowl
9¾ in. crystal spoon and fork
Eight 8½ in. crystal plates
50R-3999—1 set in carton, 15 lbs. Set 1.30

From a Butler Brothers Wholesale catalogue, Fall and Winter 1941. See Figure 151.

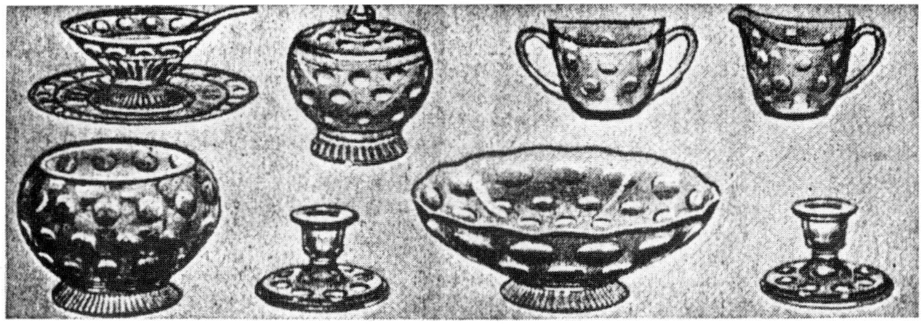

RICH RUBY GLASS ASSORTMENT

"Imperial"—Hand Made! 6 Kinds Of Pieces—Allover pressed design.
1/6 doz each of the following:

Footed Rose Bowl, 6¼ in.
Footed Fruit Bowl, 9 in.
1 pr. Candlesticks (count as 1 pc.)
Sugar and Creamer Set (count as 1 pc.)
3-Pc. Mayonnaise Set (count as 1 pc.)
Covered Candy Jar, 5½ in. high (count as 1 pc.)

50R-4576—1 doz in carton, 25 lbs. .... Doz **3.95**

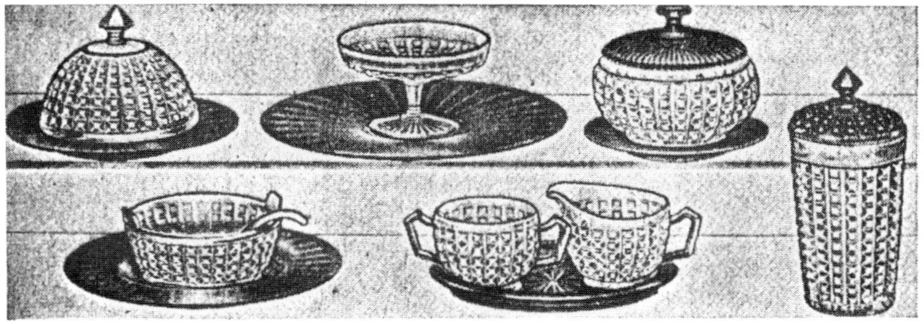

COMBINATION CRYSTAL AND RUBY GLASSWARE ASSORTMENT

"Imperial"—Hand Made!

6 Kinds Of Pieces—Exceptionally pleasing combination of rich ruby and sparkling crystal glass. These will make unusually attractive gifts. 1/6 doz each of the following:

2-Pc. Crystal Covered Candy Jar, round, 5½ in. high, ruby cover
3-Pc. Candy or Preserve Jar, 9 in. high, crystal jar, ruby cover, 6¾ in. plate.
3-Pc. Table Set, crystal sugar and creamer with 8¾ in. ruby tray
Cheese Dish, crystal cover with 9½ in. ruby tray
3-Pc. Mayonnaise Set, 5¼ in. handled crystal bowl and spoon, 8¼ in. ruby plate
2-Pc. Cheese and Cracker Set, 5¼ in. crystal tray, 10½ in. ruby tray

50R-4587—1 doz in carton, 32 lbs. .... Doz **6.00**

Glassware from Imperial Glass Corporation as shown in a Butler Brothers catalogue for January 1939. The upper assortment is in Imperial's Old English pattern. The lower assortment is the #698 Waffle Block pattern, except the candy jar lid, which is borrowed from the same company's #779 Empire pattern.

32-Pc. Crystal & Ruby Glass LUNCHEON SETS

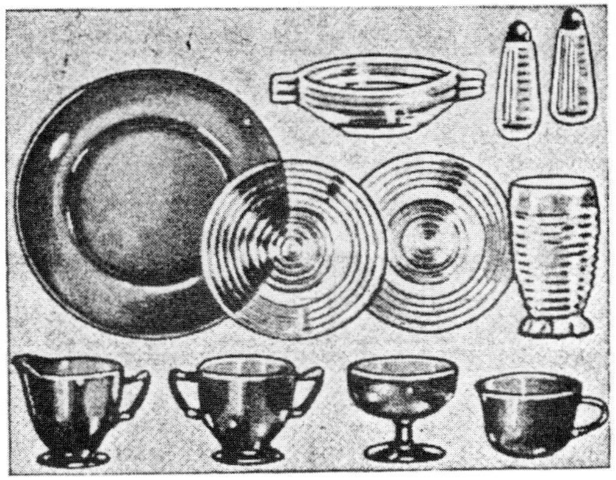

SET CONSISTS OF:
4 Ruby Cups, 3⅝x2⅝ in.
4 Crystal Saucers, 6 in.
4 Ruby Dinner Plates, 9¼ in.
4 Crystal Cream Soups, 5¼ in.
4 Ruby Sherbets, 6 oz.
4 Crystal Sherbet Plates, 6 in.
4 Crystal Tumblers, 10 oz.
1 Ruby Sugar, 3 in.
1 Ruby Creamer, 3½ in.
1 Crystal Salt With Ruby Top, 4 in.
1 Crystal Pepper With Ruby Top, 4 in.

50R-1170—1 set in carton, 21 lbs. .... Set **2.10**

Anchor Hocking glass as shown in a Butler Brothers wholesale catalogue, Summer 1940. This group continued to appear in Butler Brothers' catalogues through January 1942. See Figures 154, 156, 157, and 162.

CLEAR BLOWN GLASS IVY OR FLOWER BOWLS

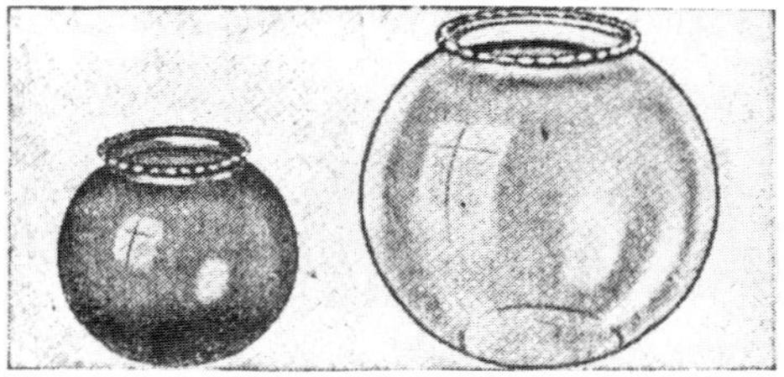

Popular Sellers
Round shapes, crimped tops. Feature them at low popular prices. They are in big demand.

4½ In. Diameter
3 doz in carton, 15 lbs.
50R-4013-1—Crystal
50R-4013-2—Ruby
Doz 45c

6 In. Diameter
3 doz in carton, 38 lbs.
50R-4033-1—Crystal
50R-4033-2—Ruby
Doz 84c

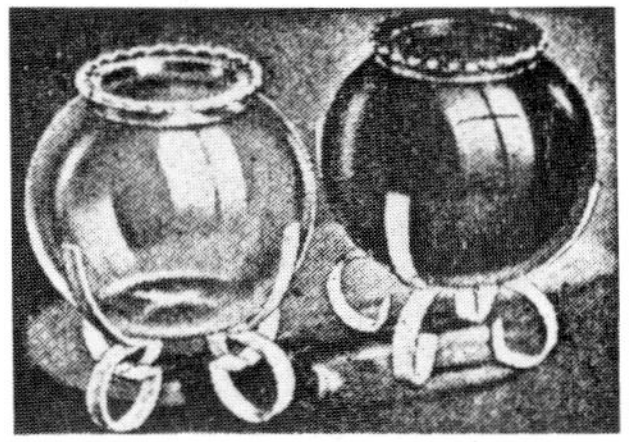

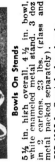

Bowls On Stands
5½ in. high overall, 4½ in. bowl, white enameled metal stand. 3 doz in 2 cartons, 23 lbs. (glass and metal packed separately).
50R-4115-1—Crystal glass bowls
50R-4115-2—Ruby glass bowls
Doz 80c

From a Butler Brothers wholesale catalogue, Fall and Winter 1941.

RUBY GLASS TABLE SPECIALTIES

Now You Can Sell These Rich Ruby Pieces At Low Popular Prices

Ruby glass is in demand. It has sold at luxury prices. Now you can offer a line of beautifully designed pieces as low as 10 cents.

Give these pieces a prominent display in your glassware and specialty lines and WATCH THEM MOVE when the customers see your price.

6½ IN. ROUND BON BON DISH
50R-4518—2 doz. in carton, 16 lbs....... Doz. .80

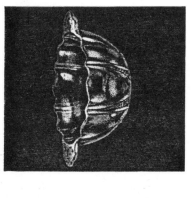

5½ IN. HANDLED DEEP SHAPE NUT BOWL
50R-4519—2 doz. in carton, 18 lbs. ...... Doz. .80

8 IN. SHALLOW MINT TRAY
50R-4523—2 doz. in carton, 23 lbs. ..... Doz. .80

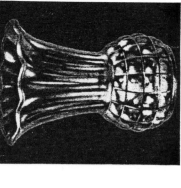

VASES

8¾ in. high, 6¼ in. diam. at top. Beautifully shaped, ideal for large bouquets. Especially adaptable to spring flowers.

50R-4055—1 doz. in carton, 25 lbs. .... Doz. 2.00

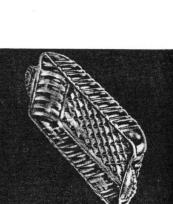

7½ IN. OBLONG RELISH DISH
50R-4524—2 doz. in carton, 19 lbs. .... Doz. .80

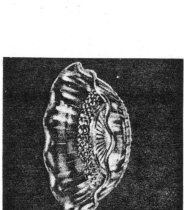

7½ IN. HANDLED MINT TRAY
50R-4521—2 doz. in carton, 18 lbs.............. Doz. .80

7 IN. THREE-TOED NAPPY
50R-4522—2 doz. in carton, 20 lbs............... Doz. .80

From a Summer 1940 catalogue of the wholesale firm Butler Brothers. See Figures 173, 175, 181, 182, and 214.

Imperial HAND MADE GIFT GLASSWARE

America's outstanding popular priced line of gift glassware!

Made by American craftsmen skilled in producing quality glassware in beautiful shapes and designs.

All pieces fully finished and brilliantly fire polished.

Assortments offered in small quantities so you can have a wide selection of styles with only a small investment.

See "Gift Glassware" in the index for pages listing our complete line of glassware for gifts. We offer many outstanding items!

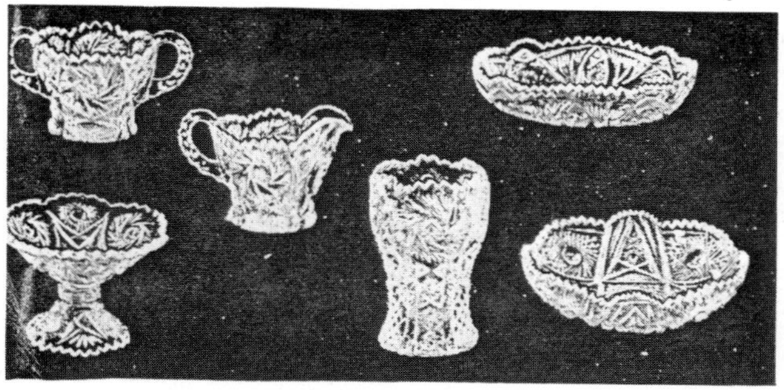

"Nu-Cut" Sparkling Heavy Crystal Glass

$2.00 DOZ

50R-4516—2 doz in carton, 40 lbs

DEEP MOLD CUT INTRICATE PATTERNS—6 KINDS OF PIECES

Hand made pieces of heavy pressed crystal in intricate design, brilliantly polished. **Asst. consists of 1/3 doz each:**

Round Bowl, 7½ in.
Oval Relish or Celery Dish, 7½ in.
Cream Pitcher, 3¾ in. high
Sugar Bowl, 3¾ in. high
Vase, 6¼ in. high
Footed Flared Comport, 5½ in.

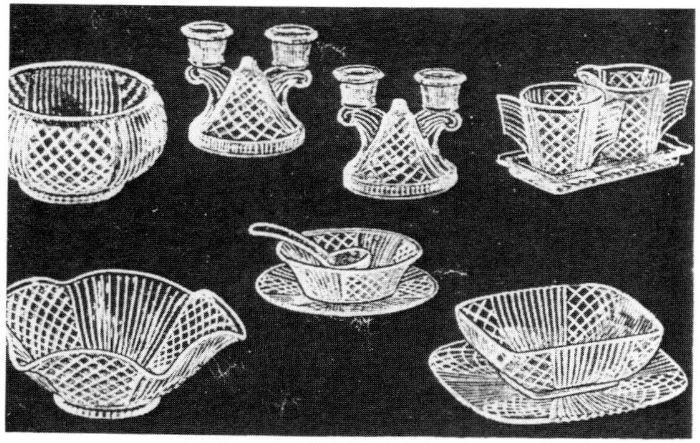

"Cristolbrite" New Jewel-Like Glass

$3.95 DOZ

50R-4541—1 doz in carton, 30 lbs

DIAMOND DESIGN WITH PRISM FLUTING—6 KINDS OF PIECES

Hand made pieces of pressed crystal with new design which combines the jewel-like appearance of diamond design with the sparkle of prism fluted design. Large sizes! **Asst. consists of 1/6 doz each:**

2-Pc. Square Salad Set of 9 in. plate & 6¾ in. bowl
3-Pc. Mayonnaise Set
3-Pc. Sugar & Creamer Set
Crimped Fruit Bowl, 10½ in.
Console or Rose Bowl, 7¼ in.
Pair of Twin Light Candle Holders, 4½ in.

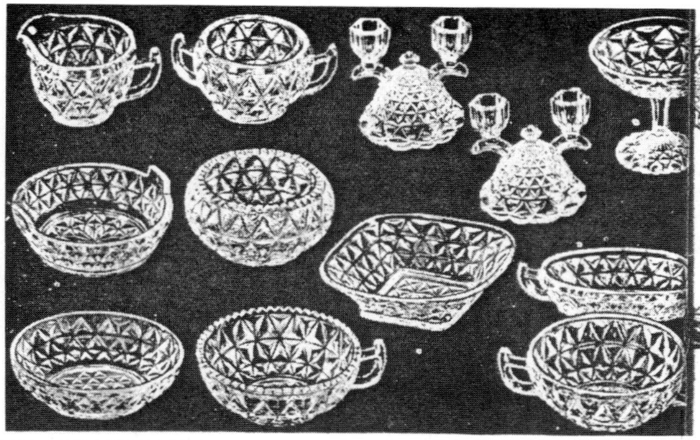

"Mt. VERNON" EARLY AMERICAN SPARKLING CRYSTAL GLASS

$1.85 DOZ

50R-4514—3 doz in carton, 38 lbs

POPULAR RE-CREATION OF COLONIAL CRYSTAL—12 KINDS OF PIECES

Hand made pieces of pressed prism design. **Asst. consists of 1/4 doz each:**

Square Nappy, 6½ in.
Round Nappy, 6¾ in.
2 Pairs Twin Light Candlesticks, 4½ in.
Ice Tub, 5¼ in.
Rose Bowl, 5½ in.
Footed Comport, 5½ in.
Creamer, 3½ in. high
Sugar, 2¾ in. high
Relish Dish, 7¾ in., double handled
Olive Dish, 6¼ in., handled
Bonbon Dish, 5¾ in., handled

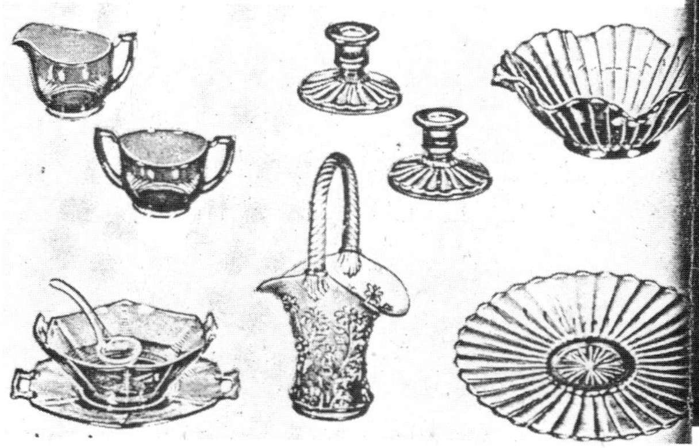

RICH AND BRILLIANT ASSORTMENT OF RUBY GLASS

$3.95 DOZ

50R-4543—1 doz in carton, 25 lbs

AN UNUSUAL OFFERING AT THIS PRICE! 6 KINDS OF PIECES

Hand made pieces of genuine ruby glass, a rich and brilliant color that sells and sells! **Asst. consists of 1/6 doz each:**

Serving Tray, 10½ in., petal design
Fruit Bowl, 9 in., petal design
Pair of Candlesticks
Handled Basket, 10 in., petal design
2-Pc. Sugar & Creamer Set
3-Pc. Mayonnaise Set

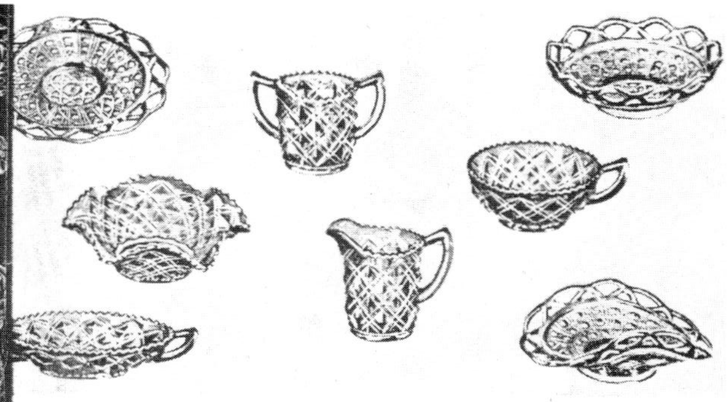

RICH RUBY GLASS IN DEEP BRILLIANT SHADE

$2.00 DOZ

50R-4515—2 doz in carton, 20 lbs

ASSTD. DIAMOND AND LACE EDGE DESIGNS—8 KINDS OF PIECES

Hand made pieces of genuine high quality ruby glass in brilliant deep shade. Asstd. diamond pressed design and delicate lace edge pieces. A big value! **Asst. consists of 1/4 doz each:**

DIAMOND PATTERN
Crimped Nut Bowl, 7 in.
Oval Relish Dish, 8 in., double handled
Round Olive Dish, 5½ in., handled
Creamer, 4 in. high
Sugar Bowl, 3½ in. high

LACE EDGE
Mint Bowl, 7 in.
Round Nappy, 6½ in.
Basket Shape Bonbon Dish, 7 in.

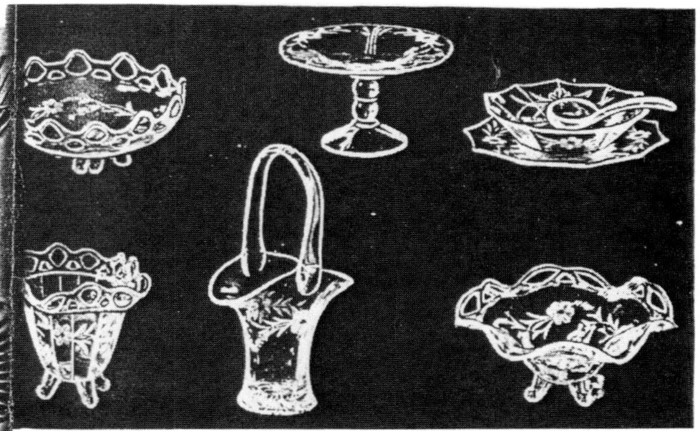

"EXQUISITE" SPARKLING CRYSTAL WITH HAND CUT DESIGN

$3.95 DOZ

50R-4540—1 doz in carton, 23 lbs

BEAUTIFUL FLORAL AND LEAF HAND CUTTING—6 KINDS OF PIECES

Hand made pieces of sparkling crystal with genuine hand cut design, some pieces with lace edge and 4 toes or feet. Asst. consists of ⅙ doz each:

Flower or Fruit Basket, 10 in. handled
Footed Flared Compote, 6¼ in.
3-Pc. Mayonnaise Set
Crimped Fruit Bowl, 8 in., lace edge
Round Fruit Bowl, 7½ in., lace edge
Crimped Top Vase, 5⅝ in., lace edge

Ruby and other glass made by Imperial Glass Corporation, as shown in a May-June 1936 catalogue of the wholesale firm Butler Brothers.

Reference Key

Richard Carter Barret's *Popular American Ruby-Stained Pattern Glass* (out-of-print)

Jerry Barnett's *Paden City — The Color Company*

Frances Bones' *The Book of Duncan Glass*

Reprint of 1930-34 Cambridge catalogues by National Cambridge Collectors, Inc.

Reprint of 1949-53 Cambridge catalogues by NCC, Inc.

Bill Edwards' *The Standard Encyclopedia of Carnival Glass* and price guide.

William Heacock's *Fenton Glass — The First 25 Years* and *Fenton Glass — The Second 25 Years*.

Gene Florence's *Depression Glass*.

Ruth Forsythe's *Made in Czechoslovakia*.

Heacock series *The Encyclopedia of Victorian Colored Pattern Glass*, Books 1-6.

Dorothy Hammond's *Confusing Collectibles* (1979 edition).

Margaret & Douglas Archer's *Imperial Glass* catalogue reprint.

Margaret James' *Black Glass*.

Minnie Kamm's series on pattern glass, Books 1-8.

Gail Krause's *The Years of Duncan*.

Gail Krause's *Duncan Glass*.

Ruth Webb Lee's *Sandwich Glass*.

Doris Lechler's *Children's Glass Dishes, China and Furniture*.

Mollie Helen McCains *The Collector's Encyclopedia of Pattern Glass*.

Marion Hartung's series on Carnival Glass, Books 1-10.

Everett & Addie Miller's two books on New Martinsville Glass Co.

Harold Newman's *An Illustrated Dictionary of Glass*.

William Heacock's *1000 Toothpick Holders*

William Heacock's *Old Pattern Glass—According to Heacock*.

Set of six *Pattern Glass Previews*, 1981 newsletter.

Arthur G. Peterson's *400 Trademarks on Glass*.

Rose Presznick's series of 4 books on *Carnival and Iridescent Glass* (out-of-print).

William Heacock's *Rare & Unlisted Toothpick Holders*.

Sandra Stout's *The Complete Book of McKee Glass*.

Sandra Stout's three color books on Depression Glass.

Clarence Vogel's set of four A. H. Heisey and Co. catalogue reprints.

Hazel Weatherman's two books on colored glass of the Depression era.

Hazel Weatherman's *Fostoria—Its First 50 Years*.

Hazel Weatherman's 1982 *Supplement & Price Trends*.

Westmoreland Specialty Co. catalogues.

Mary, Lyle & Lynn Welker's reprints of Cambridge Glass catalogues.